GOETHE

GABRIELLE BERSIER, Professor Emerita of German, Indiana University-Purdue University Indianapolis, is the author of *Wege des Heilens. Goethes physiologische Autobiographie 'Dichtung und Wahrheit'* (Koenigshausen & Neumann, 2014) and *Goethes Rätselparodie der Romantik. Eine neue Lesart der 'Wahlverwandtschaften'* (Niemeyer, 1997), along with numerous articles on Goethe's relationship with contemporary literature, art and science.

NANCY BOERNER, Librarian Emerita for German, French, Italian Languages and Literatures and Classical Studies at Indiana University-Bloomington, is the translator of Peter Boerner's biography of Goethe, first published in German in the *Rowohlts Monographien* series and subsequently in English in the *Life & Times* series (Haus, 2005 and 2015), and a number of articles.

PETER BOERNER was the curator of the Goethe Museum in Düsseldorf and later held professorships at the University of Wisconsin-Madison, SUNY-Buffalo and Indiana University. He edited the DTV paperback collection of Goethe's works in 45 volumes, and published extensively in the fields of Germanic Studies and Comparative Literature. His biography of Goethe has been translated into seven languages other than English.

GOETHE

Journeys of the Mind

Gabrielle Bersier, Nancy Boerner,
Peter Boerner

Published in 2019 by
HAUS PUBLISHING LTD
4 Cinnamon Row
London SW11 3TW

A CIP catalogue record for this book is available from the British Library

ISBN: 978-1-909961-52-4
eISBN: 978-1-909961-53-1

Typeset in Garamond by MacGuru Ltd

Printed in Spain by Liberdúplex

Contents

Preface

In response to the cliché of Goethe being a quintessential tourist, the late Peter Boerner noted that Goethe was not really a frequent traveller. Unlike his contemporaries', his actual journeys were not numerous. The list of European cities in which he never set foot is very long. Indeed, Goethe never physically visited Vienna, Paris or London, and he only once made a brief trip to Berlin, the capital of Prussia. In the last third of his life, he became essentially a homebound writer and researcher, but his intensive mental journeys counterbalanced his sedentary lifestyle. In his wide-ranging reading pursuits, Goethe conformed to the 18th-century prototype of the "armchair traveller," gaining knowledge of other countries from books and eyewitness accounts rather than from actual exploration.

When Peter Boerner began working on a monograph about Goethe as an armchair traveller, he was already weakened by the illness that finally took his life on 12 June 2015. He had developed an outline of the book and had written its introduction, as well as leaving behind a number of related essays that became the cornerstone of the present study. At his request, we continued on the path that he had set and expanded his original design to include additional destinations, focusing on the crystallisation of Goethe's reading journeys into literary, scientific and artistic adventures.

The present book, *Goethe: Journeys of the Mind,* is dedicated to Peter Boerner's memory.

Indianapolis and Bloomington, 30 June 2018
Gabrielle Bersier Nancy Boerner

Introduction

The renowned German author Johann Wolfgang von Goethe was born on 28 August 1749 in Frankfurt am Main, a bustling commercial city. He died on 22 March 1832 in Weimar, the seat of a small German duchy. During his lifetime, with only horses or ships to rely on to cover long distances, few people had an opportunity to travel. Yet many were able to discover distant locations by reading about them.

Without ever leaving their homes, and needing no passport, these readers could share the experience of travelling and form opinions about various parts of the world based on what they learned from the accounts of others. Their backgrounds and interests varied considerably: they could be young or old, male or female and from any station in life. They might read to increase their knowledge, to participate vicariously in their informants' adventures or simply to indulge in, as one journal title put it, "geographical diversions." Some of these stay-at-home travellers enjoyed learning about far-off places in the company of friends, others withdrew to read in solitude. As they never personally saw the places they read about, the English called them "armchair" or "fireside" travellers.

In the diversity and intensity of their interests, the armchair travellers of the time may have been almost as well informed as those who had undertaken the journeys themselves. Both types of travellers proceeded from a multitude of individual observations to form more general conclusions. Readers, like their guides, may at times have focused their studies only on certain aspects of a foreign country, for example on economic, political or scientific issues. The broader their educational background, the more they were able to absorb information about many varied topics.

In accordance with their own particular interests, armchair travellers synthesised the information that came to them through different channels in order to construct images of countries and peoples. By comparing a number of sources and weighing them against each other, they gained insights into foreign cultures that were often scarcely less perceptive than those of the original travellers. Those experiences – as Goethe observed in his *Italienische Reise* (*Italian Journey*), recounting an 18-month stay in Italy – could be contingent on "purpose, conditions at the time and the auspiciousness or unfavourability of the circumstances." Daniel Defoe even claimed that readers of travel accounts who had circled the globe with William Dampier and Woodes Rogers had learned a thousand times more than many a sailor who couldn't read.

To judge from the prefaces to various travel reports, authors often were aware of their potential audience even as they began their journeys. While writing their accounts they kept this audience in mind and respected its critical authority, recognising the significance of the vicarious journey as a complement to the actual one. Knowing that their work would be read by many armchair travellers influenced the reporting of authors such as Goethe's contemporary Karl Philipp Moritz, who felt they were mediators between foreign cultures and that of their home country.

Goethe, like other armchair travellers of his time, had available a number of sources for his journeys, from detailed travel guides and reports to statistical surveys and histories, as well as descriptions of life in the literature of other countries. Newly published travel accounts and contact with actual travellers made it possible to renew and update the armchair traveller's knowledge.

Almost daily throughout his life, Goethe spent many hours studying novels, plays and poetry, philosophical treatises and scientific essays. Not least, he also read travel narratives from many parts of the world (see Figure 1).

He began to travel through the medium of books in his early youth. As he recalled later in his autobiography *Dichtung und Wahrheit* (*Poetry and Truth*), his father owned a collection of the "best and newest travel reports" and urged the boy to immerse himself in them. An account of the circumnavigation of the globe from 1740 to 1744 by the British naval officer Lord George Anson was one of the first books with which he became acquainted.[1] While accompanying "this outstanding sailor" in his mind, Goethe absorbed the "value of truth" along with the "imagination of fairy tales."

Goethe remained interested in the study of travel

accounts throughout his life. As well as travel literature per se, he read geographical and historical handbooks, literature that described life in other nations and scientific works from all over the world. In addition, many notable travellers provided him with information, either in letters, in unpublished materials or in person.

The extent of his reading can be illustrated by his own library: the sections "Geography" and "Travels" list more than 200 titles, among them atlases, statistical analyses and ethnographic compendia.[2] He also borrowed many books on other parts of the world from the ducal library in Weimar, which records that between 1799 and 1831 over 300 volumes related to travels were lent out to him.[3]

In addition to his reading, Goethe gleaned much information from the numerous visitors who came to see him in Weimar. He enjoyed questioning scientists, scholars, artists and other travellers about what they had observed and experienced. As an armchair traveller, he thus could acquire a more extensive breadth of information than he would have by travelling on his own. He claimed, not without justification, that travel accounts helped him to "see the world clearly."

Though there is value in a quantitative assessment of the travel publications that interested Goethe, or of the number of travellers with whom he came into contact, it is the content of what he read and what he heard from others that is far more interesting, as this helped him form vivid images not only of specific places but also of countries and peoples.

Goethe as Traveller and as Stay-at-Home

During his life Goethe enthusiastically undertook several journeys that proved to be central to his development. The foremost example is his 18-month stay in Italy, where he left behind his administrative duties for the ducal court in Weimar in order to be able to devote himself completely to learning about Italy, its art and its culture, and to taking up his literary work again. Three visits to Switzerland and, in his later years, two visits to the Rhine and Main River areas, were also formative. Over the years, many publications have invited readers to follow in his "footsteps" in a variety of landscapes.

His travel experiences enabled him to compare his own observations with the opinions prevalent among his contemporaries about each country and its people. For example, during a visit to Naples in May 1787, using a guidebook penned by Johann Jacob Volkmann, *Historisch-kritische Nachrichten von Italien, welche eine genaue Beschreibung dieses Landes, der Sitten und Gebräuche… enthalten. Aus den neuesten französischen und englischen Reisebeschreibungen und aus eignen Anmerkungen zusammengetragen*[4] (*Historical-critical information about Italy, including… a detailed description of the country, its customs and traditions. Compiled from the most recent French and English travel accounts and personal observations*), Goethe read about the laziness of the inhabitants of the city. In his first days there, however, he had not seen any idlers at all, and he hesitated to give credence to this depiction without determining for himself how the residents spent their days. What particularly bothered him, as he recounted later in his autobiographical *Italian Journey*, was Volkmann's assertion that there were 40,000 *Lazzaroni*, or knaves, in Naples, "shiftless folk who have no real jobs."[5] But Goethe had not observed such people. Acquaintances, asked about the discrepancy, did not know of any either. Thus, Goethe recounted, he "took up the hunt" himself. For days he closely observed Neapolitans of all kinds, including shopkeepers, artisans, porters, fishermen and beggars, but he could not find any who were not going about some kind of daily pursuit. He finally concluded that the people of Naples were no less industrious than any others, and that anything derogatory that was said about them was based on ignorance. Volkmann's view of them, he decided, must have been reached from a "northern perspective that considers anyone an idler who does not slog anxiously all day long."

On another occasion he observed that "the English are accused of bringing their teakettles with them everywhere they go, even to the top of Mount Etna; but do not all nations have their teakettles in which, when travelling, they brew their own bundles of herbs brought from home?" Goethe later remarked that one of the benefits he gained from his experiences in Italy, in addition to an understanding of art and art history, was a growing interest in studying the customs of various nations. As an armchair traveller, he pursued this interest for his entire life.

Goethe's sojourn in Italy was not the last time he visited another country, but it was the only journey in which he became well acquainted with an entire nation. A trip to northeastern France, undertaken at the request of his patron and friend Duke Carl August of Sachsen-Weimar-Eisenach, to observe a campaign led by the armies of Austrian and German monarchs against Jacobin France, as well as trips to Bohemian spas, were more limited in purpose. Thus, in the more than 40 years after his return from Italy, the information he acquired about other countries was generally not based on his own personal experience. He read the equivalent of a whole library of foreign works of literature, either in the original language or in translation, not only by authors from Western nations, but also by writers from Eastern Europe, the Middle East and Asia. In the course of his scientific studies, he utilised Italian, French and English sources in addition to German ones. As a passionate armchair traveller, he was familiar with published accounts about many parts of the world, and a wide-ranging correspondence, along with his many visitors, kept him abreast of new developments. What he learned about other lands is reflected to a greater or lesser extent in much of his work, especially in his literary and scientific writings.

A characteristic feature of Goethe's own travels was his habit, one can almost call it an obsession, to put his experiences into written form. His methods of presentation were varied. A published account of his first trip to Switzerland was an edited version of his spontaneous notes. His *Italian Journey* was based on a careful re-reading and editing of the letters he wrote to his friends in Weimar while he was away. An account of his travels in the Rhine, Main and Neckar river areas was written during his visits there.

Goethe's more extensive journeys came to an end in the summer of 1816. On 20 July, having set off in the direction of Erfurt on a planned third trip to the Rhine and Main areas, Goethe and a companion found their journey summarily interrupted. Goethe described the event in a letter of 22 July to Grand Duchess Louise, declaring that he was no longer going to continue with his original plans but instead, on the advice of his doctor, would spend the remainder of the "best month of the year" at a nearby spa in Bad Tennstedt:

> I left here at 7 in the morning; at 9, shortly before Münchenholzen, the clumsiest of all drivers capsized the carriage, the axle broke and the good Mr. Meyer [his travelling companion] sustained a gash to his forehead. The heavy bleeding of the wound was a problem, but we clambered out of the coach as best we could. All we could do was send for help from Weimar, which arrived after several hours that fortunately we were able to spend out in the open under a sunny sky.

Almost 67 at the time, and beginning to notice signs of his own aging, Goethe took the accident to be a warning from Providence and decided no longer to subject himself to the exertions of protracted travels. After the carriage was repaired, he used it only for travelling in the area around Weimar and Jena, as well as for relatively short trips to enjoy curative sojourns at spas in Bohemia, to which his coach brought him via familiar routes (see

Figure 2). He declined invitations to be an honoured guest in places such as Vienna and, in response to friends in Berlin who repeatedly entreated him to undertake the two-day journey to the city, he explained that he had to use the time remaining to him to pursue his work as an author and scientist in his accustomed environment.

The turning point in Goethe's life caused by the carriage accident did not, however, preclude all travel experiences. On the contrary, if not in person, he could still travel vicariously, and indeed he became an even more enthusiastic traveller of the mind than he had been an adventurous explorer in earlier years.

Journeys to England

England was the non-German-speaking country that Goethe knew best from a variety of vicarious experiences, although he never set foot in it. Germans of the late 18th century had an array of resources at their disposal, from literary descriptions and exhaustive travel guides to statistics on living conditions in various areas of the country. From newly published reports and from descriptions of English life in contemporary novels, as well as from personal contact with British travellers who came to Weimar, Goethe was able to reinforce and expand his knowledge about the country. Even though he had never been there, he formed his own picture of the unseen land and its inhabitants. With his wide-ranging interests and his ability to process diverse ideas, he developed a broad panorama of knowledge about England.

Beginning at an early age, Goethe had absorbed many lasting impressions about Britain from his own reading. As a boy he became familiar, for example, with British journals, Jonathan Swift's *Gulliver's Travels*, Alexander Pope's writings and the novels of Samuel Richardson. As a student in Leipzig, he was influenced by George Lillo's *The London Merchant*, probably also early on by

Thomas Gray's churchyard poetry, Edward Young's *Night Thoughts* and Thomas Percy's *Folio of Old English Ballads and Romances*. Later, while studying in Strasbourg, he began to read Sterne, Goldsmith, Ossian and Shakespeare. His impressions of British life gained from these seemingly "just literary" sources are recounted in his autobiography *Poetry and Truth*: at one point he notes that during a visit he made from Strasbourg to a parsonage in the small town of Sesenheim, he realised with amused surprise how similar the members of the pastor's family were to characters described in Oliver Goldsmith's *The Vicar of Wakefield*. Another time, he talks about the fascination Shakespeare held for his circle of friends in Strasbourg:

> Shakespeare pervaded our group, translated and in the original, as a whole or in excerpts, to such an extent that, just as there are men well versed in the Bible, we gradually became immersed in Shakespeare and in our conversations reconstructed the virtues and failings of his time with which he had made us familiar; we had a lot of fun with his quibbles by trying to translate them, and also mischievously vied with him.

Much later in his life, in a letter to his friend Carl Friedrich Zelter of 5 October 1830, Goethe remarked about Sterne's *Tristram Shandy*: "With the years my admiration heightens; for who else in the year 1759 recognised pedantry and philistinism so exquisitely and described them with such hilarity? I still don't know of his equal in any book circles."

In addition to impressions he gained from literature, personal experiences starting in his youth awakened and stimulated Goethe's interest in England. As a 12-year-old, he learned the rudiments of English from a doctoral candidate in theology who was one of the first people in Germany to give instruction in the language. Subsequently, the youth became acquainted with some young Britons who were living in Frankfurt to further their business education. Around 1764, he and his sister often saw one of them in particular, Harry Lupton, the son of a London cloth merchant. In his later years, Goethe remembered that Lupton was able "to use his language ably," and that from him the siblings had learned "many things about his land and people."

Goethe's language exercises were clearly not unsuccessful, as is evident from letters he wrote from Leipzig in English to his sister Cornelia. His father had wanted to see if he could express himself competently in the language. On 11 May 1766 he wrote the following passage, in which the spelling and usage are his own:

> Any words of my self: Sister I am a foolish boy. Thou
> knowst it; why should I say it? My soul is changed a
> little. I am no more a thunderer as I was at Francfort.
> I make no more: J'enrage. I am as meek! as meek!
> Hah thou believest it not! Many a time I become
> a melancholical one. I know not whence it comes.
> Then I look on every man with a starring owl like

countenance. Then I go in woods, to streams, I look on the pyed daisies on the blue violets, I hear the nightingales, the larks, the rooks and daws, the cuckow; And then a darkness comes down my soul; a darkness as thik as fogs in the October are… In like a situation of my soul, I make english verses… that a stone would weep. In that moment thou shalt have of them. Think on it sister thou art a happy maiden, to have a brother who makes English verses. I pray thee, be not haughty thereof.

A Song
over
The Unconfidence
toward my self
To Dr. Schlosser

Thou knowst how happily they Freind
  Walks upon florid Ways;
Thou knowst how heavens bounteous hand
  Leads him to golden days.

But hah! a cruel enemy
  Destroies all that Bless;
In Moments of Melancholy
  Flies all my Happiness.

Then fogs of doubt do fill my mind
  With deep obscurity;
I search my self, and cannot find

A spark of Worth in me.

When tender friends, to tender kiss,
Run up with open arms;
I think I merit not that bliss,
That like a kiss me warmeth.

Hah! when my child, I love thee, sayd
And gave the kiss I sought;
Then I – forgive me tender maid –
She is a false one, thought.

She cannot love a peevish boy,
She with her godlike face.
O could I, freind, that t[h]ought destroy,
It leads the golden days.

And other t[h]ought is misfortune
Is death and night to me:
I hum no supportable tune,
I can no poet be.

When to the Altar of the Nine
A triste incense I bring;
I beg let Poetry be mine,
O Sistres, let me sing.

But when they then my prayer not hear,
I break my wispring lire;
Then from my eyes runns down a tear,

Extinguish th' incensed fire.

Then curse I, Freind, the fated sky,
And from th' altar I fly;
And to my Freinds aloud I cry,
Be happier than I.

Are they not beautifull sister? Ho yes! Senza Dubbio.

Although this and other English poems he composed at the time may seem clumsy to the practised eye, they demonstrate that, at the age of 17, he was sufficiently competent to express himself in the language, an ability he retained into his old age.

After his move from Frankfurt to Weimar in 1775, at the invitation of Duke Carl August, Goethe continued to gain knowledge of England, mainly from his contact with the British agronomist George Batty. Appointed by Carl August to serve as his Superintendent of Agriculture and charged with overseeing agricultural improvements, especially the draining of marshy areas, Batty became one of the few court officials whom Goethe trusted completely as he carried out his own administrative duties. The extent of this trust – and the confidence it engendered in him – is expressed in a number of Goethe's diary entries in July 1779. Batty appears in them as a model for everything that his admirer wished to achieve, as when he noted that a master of his craft "goes right to what needs to be done, like Batty on a country estate; he doesn't have dreams in general terms, like I did about becoming an artist. If he has to get something done, he does exactly what is needed."

Later, during his sojourn in Italy from 1786 to 1788, Goethe spent many hours in Rome with Karl Philipp Moritz, author of *Reisen eines Deutschen in England im Jahr 1782*[1] (*Travels of a German in England in the Year 1782*), who recounted what he had experienced during his lengthy travels around England four years previously. While in Italy, Goethe also frequently socialised with Englishmen living there, such as the painter and art dealer Thomas Jenkins, whose urbane manner he admired, and William Hamilton, the British envoy in Naples, who was a patron and supporter of archaeological excavations in Herculaneum, and who seemed to the German visitor to be a master of the art of elegant living.

Following his return to Germany, Goethe continued to have many opportunities to cultivate personal contacts with Britons. As had been the case in Italy, he was impressed by their ease in social situations. He developed a close connection to Charles Gore, a merchant of considerable wealth who had taken up permanent residence in Weimar. After Gore's death, Goethe recalled that he had always made "a kindly impression," and because he "had seen, experienced and read a good deal, one can indeed say he spent no moment of his life on insignificant matters." Goethe felt that conversations with Gore were never short on substance.

After the Napoleonic wars, Goethe came in contact with a growing number of Englishmen who visited Weimar. In general, as Johann Peter Eckermann – one of his trusted assistants – noted on 12 March 1828, Goethe found that the British visitors comported themselves with "total confidence," and "they behaved as comfortably as if they were at home everywhere." They were mainly young men who had come to view with their own eyes the haunts of German writers whom they revered: Goethe, Schiller, Herder and Wieland. Catering to these visitors became a profitable "industry" in the city: guesthouses and boarding schools were opened, and many a local intellectual, including Eckermann, was able to stay afloat by offering language lessons. Goethe was in a position to observe these developments at close range, as his daughter-in-law Ottilie was the impetus behind many of the receptions and balls held for foreigners. Parsimonious with his time, the author found these activities burdensome, but consoled himself by learning from the guests; if one knows how to take advantage of such visits, he pointed out to Eckermann, "in the end" they convey "a sense of the nation," indeed "of three nations, as it were," if the Scots and the Irish were included.

Goethe observed the self-assured demeanour of the young guests from England:

> Whether it is due to their ancestry, their native soil, their open disposition, their healthy upbringing – whatever it is, the English in general appear to have an advantage over many others. Here in Weimar we see only a small number of them and probably not necessarily the best ones, but they are all capable and good-looking people indeed! And even as young as

> they are when they travel here, even at seventeen years of age, they don't feel strange and ill at ease in this foreign German environment; on the contrary, their appearance and their behaviour in public is as confident and easy as if they were the lords of everyone and owned the entire world. That appeals to our ladies as well, and wreaks much havoc in the hearts of our young damsels. As a German paterfamilias who likes his peace, I often feel a slight pang of dread when my daughter-in-law announces the imminent arrival of some new young islander. I can already imagine the tears that will flow at his future departure. They are venturesome young people; but of course, that they are venturesome is also their virtue.

Eckermann demurred somewhat: "Nonetheless I would not like to claim, I replied, that the young Englishmen in our Weimar are brighter, more sophisticated, better educated and more admirable at heart than other people." Goethe answered:

> That is not what matters. Their birth and wealth don't matter, either; what does matter is that they have the courage to be as Nature has made them. They are not over-sophisticated or warped, they don't deal in half-measures or falseness; whatever they do, they are always complete individuals.

One of the young Britons who visited Weimar was William Makepeace Thackeray, later known for his novel

Vanity Fair and many other works (see Figure 3). At the age of 19, after visiting Paris, Thackeray arrived in Weimar and remained there from autumn 1830 to spring 1831, occasionally being invited to tea by Goethe or his daughter-in-law Ottilie, even though he was not yet well known.

Goethe also received much encouragement from Duke Carl August to deal with English matters. Towards the end of the Napoleonic wars, the Duke had become an obsessed Anglophile, and in 1814 he undertook a lengthy trip to England, where the lifestyle of London society, especially the mutual respect between the nobility and the bourgeoisie, deeply impressed him. He became a member of the English Botanical Society and was able to obtain thousands of plants from Kew Gardens for the ducal park in Tiefurt near Weimar. After his return, he sought to help his duchy profit from Britain's technological expertise by experimenting with a technique developed by the Scots engineer McAdam of building straight roads that were called "chaussées." Constructed by engineers to be slightly convex, so that rainwater drained off them easily, they were paved with tightly packed small stones and gravel, compacted into a hard surface. The Duke also installed Germany's first gas lamps on the streets of Weimar. Carl August's projects were of considerable interest to Goethe, not least because he could connect them to his own scientific studies. Although in general he spent only a small amount of time with journals and magazines, he carefully perused *The Foreign Quarterly Review* and *The Edinburgh Review* to keep abreast of developments in Britain. He also had access to the extensive dossiers sent by a German translator in the Foreign Office, Johann Christian Hüttner, who acted as an agent of the Weimar court in London.

However, Goethe's continued attention to books concerning England remained of greater consequence than all these personal contacts. His early interest in English literature remained with him for the rest of his life. Time and again, in both his poetic and critical writings, he grappled with Shakespeare. He was just as open to newer authors, and read in particular the works of Scott, Shelley, Moore and Burns. Byron, he felt, was the most accomplished talent among his contemporaries. And he learned with pleasure in 1827 that Thomas Carlyle, author of *The Life of Friedrich Schiller: Comprehending an Examination of His Works*,[2] wished to initiate contact with him. At Goethe's suggestion, the work was translated by members of the Gesellschaft für ausländische schöne Literatur in Berlin (Berlin Society for Foreign Literatures). It was published in 1830, with a 20-page introduction by Goethe.

He was similarly pleased when in 1831 Carlyle arranged for 15 prominent British authors and intellectuals to send him a birthday gift as an indication of the high esteem in which he was held in England. A letter of their appreciation was accompanied by a seal made of nephrite, gold and enamel into which was engraved Goethe's maxim "Ohne Hast, ohne Rast" ("Without haste, without rest"). Goethe expressed his gratitude in a poem, "Den funfzehn Englischen Freunden" ("To the Fifteen English Friends") (see Figure 4), that he wrote on his birthday and sent off in an envelope closed with red wax, stamped by the birthday seal:

Den funfzehn Englischen Freunden	To the fifteen English friends
Worte, die der Dichter spricht,	Words uttered by the author
Treu, in heimischen Bezirken,	Ring true in his native land,
Wirken gleich, doch weiß er nicht	But he knows not
Ob sie in die Ferne wirken.	Whether they are understood abroad.
Britten! habt sie aufgefaßt:	You British! have taken them in:
"Tätigen Sinn, das Tun gezügelt;	"An active mind, restrained activity;
Stetig Streben, ohne Hast."	Continuously striving, without haste."
Und so wollt Ihr's denn besiegelt.	And thus you wished to seal it.

Weimar 28. August 1831. J. W. Goethe

Other publications to which Goethe also directed his attention discussed political and social life in England, as well as its history and geography. Chief among them were contemporary travel accounts. In the course of his life, Goethe read about 30 works that fell into this category, some of them quite voluminous. Most of them corresponded to his preference to inform himself by studying factual descriptions, such as the *Neueste Reise durch England, Schottland und Ireland, hauptsächlich in bezug auf Produkte, Fabriken und Handlung*[3] (*Most Recent Journey through England, Scotland and Ireland, Particularly with Reference to Products, Factories and Business*) by Philipp Andreas Nemnich; the six-volume *Voyages dans la Grande-Bretagne, entrepris relativement aux services publics de la guerre, de la marine, et des ponts et chaussées, au commerce et à l'industrie, depuis 1816*[4] (*Travels Undertaken in Great Britain Relating to the Public Services of War, the Navy, Bridges and Chaussées, Commerce and Industry, since 1816*) by Charles Dupin; and Heinrich Meidinger's *Reisen durch Großbritannien und Irland vorzüglich in topographischer, kommerzieller und statistischer Hinsicht: Neuestes Handbuch für Reisende durch die drei vereinigten Königreiche England, Schottland und Irland*[5] (*Travels through Great Britain and Ireland, Mainly Concerning Topography, Commerce and Statistics: Most Recent Handbook for Travellers in the Three United Kingdoms of England, Scotland and Ireland*). It is possible to document when and under what conditions Goethe dealt with almost each one of these works. Concerning Nemnich, for example, he noted in his diary on 4 August, 1807, "Arrival of Nemnich's new journey. Cut it open and read quite a bit in it." Dupin's work, a large-format edition with numerous lithographs, was frequently the object of his attention, and he corresponded with Sulpiz Boisserée, a collector and art historian, about it. Johanna Schopenhauer's three-volume memoir about her trip to England, France and the Netherlands, *Erinnerungen von einer Reise in den Jahren 1803, 1804 und 1805*[6]

(*Recollections of a Journey in the Years 1803, 1804 and 1805*), was of particular interest to him because he had a close personal connection to the famous Weimar author, who was mother to the philosopher Arthur Schopenhauer.

Goethe's interest in England did not flag, even in the last months before his death. He wrote a long review of a collection of travel letters penned by Prince Hermann von Pückler-Muskau and published anonymously by the Prince's wife (while he was still very much alive) as *Briefe eines Verstorbenen: Ein fragmentarisches Tagebuch aus England, Wales, Irland und Frankreich, geschrieben in den Jahren 1826–29*[7] (*Letters of a Dead Man: A Fragmentary Diary from England, Wales, Ireland and France Written in the Years 1826–29*). Goethe's praise of the lively style of the travelogue played a decisive role in its success. His characterisation of the writer's ability to produce word paintings gives us a sense of Goethe's own expectations of a well-written landscape depiction that could almost substitute for real travels:

> Descriptions of the scenery comprise the main content of the letters, but these are admirably successful. England, Wales, particularly Ireland and then again the north coast of England are portrayed masterfully. One can't help but think that he had the subject directly in front of him as he rendered it with his pen; for even if he conscientiously wrote in his epistolary diary every evening, such a clear and detailed depiction is still a rare phenomenon.

Goethe was still devoting time to Pückler-Muskau's letters in March 1832, the month of his death.

In addition to perusing descriptive travel reports for information about England and English affairs, Goethe was also very interested in the work of British scholars and often made use of their publications in his many scientific writings, especially with regard to optics and geology. Always at hand in his study was George Greenough's *Critical Examination of the First Principles of Geology*, an exhaustive treatise on the rock formations of the British Isles.[8] England's climatic conditions were familiar to him from the works of Luke Howard, a London meteorologist, who also provided him with the methodological basis for his own studies of clouds. Goethe's occupation with Newton's theory of colour ultimately led him to extensive research on the natural sciences in England from the time of Roger Bacon to his own day. He studied in detail the four-volume *History of the Royal Society of London* with its numerous references to societal conditions in the country.[9] How central England was to his investigations of the physical world is documented in his *Zur Farbenlehre. Historischer Teil* (*History of the Theory of Colours*): no fewer than 23 of the 72 chapters in the section on the 18th century refer to developments in Britain.

The knowledge that Goethe acquired from the resources available to him concerning artistic, geographic, political, social, economic and scientific matters in England must have been considerable. He knew, for example, where basalt could be found in the British Isles, and he could describe the floor plan of Buckingham Palace; he could converse about English agriculture and garden art, about London linen factories, about the East India Company and even about different types of British military weapons and armaments.

Goethe's Understanding of the English Character

The images of specific peoples that armchair travellers of the 18th and 19th centuries delineated for themselves often included opinions about their "national character." When Goethe spoke of the English people, he did not base his remarks only on various general statements about the psychology of nations made by Montaigne, Hume or Kant; he knew that he was in the company of many of his friends who, themselves armchair travellers, had come to similar conclusions. Thus, also without setting foot on British soil, his compatriot Johann Caspar Lavater in his *Physiognomische Fragmente zur Beförderung der Menschenkenntniß und Menschenliebe*[10] (*Physiognomic Fragments Concerning the Advancement of Human Nature and Humanitarianism*) felt that he could voice opinions about the attributes of the English character based on their physical appearance. Furthermore, simply on the basis of his reading experiences, Johann Gottfried Herder spoke confidently of the purposefulness of the English in both private and business affairs as a specific feature of their character.

Following his inclination to proceed whenever possible from the specific to the general, Goethe consolidated all the diverse information he had acquired into a cultural overview. The keyword for this kind of cultural image can be recognised in his notion of national character: while careful to avoid stereotypes, he tended, as did his contemporaries, to see the people of a nation as a balanced organism distinguished by specific characteristics influenced by climatic and historical conditions. Similar to an individual person, each nation had its strengths and weaknesses, virtues and faults.

Goethe's frequent remarks about England in his autobiographical and scientific writings, as well as in notes jotted down later by some of those with whom he conversed or corresponded, indicate he felt that the cardinal virtue of the English was their practicality. As he had observed about the agronomist Batty, they always did "just what needs to be done, what is necessary at the time; they are people who are focused on realities." Because they generally wished to present themselves "as nature made them," they always seemed "entirely complete persons" who possessed a "pure common sense" and knew how to differentiate "the useful from the useless."

Where did Britons get this affinity for the real and the natural? According to Goethe, the explanation could be found in their geographical situation. Due to their island existence, which separated them from other peoples, they had always been motivated to go to sea, to develop a trading network, to explore the whole world. The vast expanses of the sea had given them a broadmindedness of spirit. Thus he spoke of Shakespeare's England as a nation "active in all regions of the world." He claimed that because the third Earl of Shaftesbury, an English politician, writer and philosopher, lived "surrounded by the sea," he was able to achieve more than the prominent German literary author of the Enlightenment, Christoph Martin Wieland, who had no opportunities to absorb the world, living as he did in a provincial part of the continent. Similarly, Goethe felt that the empirical philosopher and scientist Francis Bacon eclipsed his German counterpart, geologist and mineralogist Georgius Agricola, because as a member of a nation that had to cooperate with the entire world, Bacon was always "compelled by external circumstances to deal with the far-reaching and infinite."

Wherever in the world the English settled, Goethe asserted in his *History of the Theory of Colours*, they radiated a feeling of "personal steadiness, sureness and activity," of "self-confidence" and "prosperity." This good fortune of the English had an important consequence: literary and scientific activities in England – different from those in Germany – were undertaken not just by a few individuals, but by many in a broad stratum of society. Shakespeare was able to be so productive because he could count on a general interest in his works and because he came at the "right harvest time." Robert Burns had a "lively grass-roots following, which allowed him to make further strides," and the work of the Royal Society was so successful because all sections of the people – the king, the nobility, scholars, economists, journeymen, merchants and craftsmen – were interested and involved in it. In the sciences, too, the English demonstrated the same sense of community and enterprise that they had developed on the seas. "The Briton is a master at making immediate use of discoveries, which leads to new discoveries and action,"

Goethe asserted in his *Maximen und Reflexionen* (*Maxims and Reflections*).

In contrast to other nations, the English gave Goethe few grounds for criticism. What did irritate him, however, was the tendency toward melancholy that could be recognised in some 18th-century British authors, such as Young, Gray and Sterne. Much of their writing, he maintained in his autobiography *Poetry and Truth*, was accompanied by an earnest gloominess, which was communicated to everyone who studied their work. It is necessary to note here, however, that in his later years, Goethe reacted negatively not only to the culture of world-weariness prevalent among some English authors, but also to his own former connection to it. In his earlier closeness to the melancholy mood of these writers, as well as in his ability to comprehend this mood even in his old age, one can perhaps detect a basis for his deep understanding of English literature. Indicative of this are the thorough discussion of English pre-romantic writers that he included in his autobiography and his affinity for Lord Byron, who reminded him of his own youthful escapades.

As Madame de Staël had done with reference to her French compatriots in her book *De l'Allemagne*[11] (*On Germany*), Goethe used his observations of the English to contrast them with the inhabitants of his own nation. Especially as he grew older and distanced himself increasingly from political and literary developments in Germany, he frequently pointed to the English as the representatives of a possible alternative approach. He contrasted their habit of always starting with whatever was most necessary, with the manner in which the Germans conducted their lives. The latter, it seemed to him, lacked a "breadth of view": instead of being immersed "in worldly activities" as were the "energetic" English, they plagued themselves "with solving philosophical problems."

Thus, like many armchair travellers who found that their vicarious journeys offered them an opportunity not only to broaden their factual knowledge, but also to shape their own character, when Goethe repeatedly spoke of the dynamism of the English, he did so because he felt the Germans should emulate them in this respect. His readiness to ascribe a pedagogical impact to travel reports corresponded to the thinking of the time, which is confirmed by other authors. Swift's patron William Temple, for example, declared that from reading descriptions of foreign countries, one comes to understand how many moral principles are common to all peoples. The 18th-century scientist and writer Albrecht von Haller even claimed that an individual's knowledge of himself is "due in large part to travellers," because in reading their reports, one gains experiences to which one would not otherwise be privy:

> We are enriched with a thousand useful truths; we discard our prejudices, and we enjoy the fruit of the grave dangers and protracted efforts undergone by other men, who worked on our behalf at various times and in various places.

Goethe's Poetic Journey to the Orient

The Hafez–Goethe memorial in Beethoven Square in Weimar was unveiled in 2000 by Presidents Sayyed Mohammad Khatami of Iran and Johannes Rau of Germany. Designed by Ernst Thevis and Fabian Rabsch, the monument displays two granite chairs facing each other in opposing, east–west directions. Both pieces are carved in such a way that they form two halves of a whole that can be joined into one single stone block (see Figure 5).

At the foot of the monument a "ghazal" – or love poem – by Hafez is inscribed in Persian calligraphy within a web of decorative patterns and is juxtaposed with Goethe's verse:

Wer sich selbst und andere kennt,	Who knows himself and others well
Wird auch hier erkennen:	No longer may ignore:
Orient und Okzident	Orient and Occident
Sind nicht mehr zu trennen.	Are separate no more.[1]

This visual celebration of the boundary-erasing, unifying force of poetry embodies one of the goals of Goethe's *West–Östlicher Divan* (*West-East Divan*), in its literal translation from the Persian a "collection," or gathering, of oriental poems, intended to kindle Western interest in Islamic culture and literature. Two centuries after it was met with indifference by the German reading public of its time, the *West-East Divan* has today gained a new level of contemporary relevance in a world replete with ethnic and religious conflicts.

Perhaps none of Goethe's journeys of the mind had as great an influence on his writings as his discovery of the collection of medieval Persian songs, or *Diwan*, of Mohammad Schemsed-din Hafez, which he read in their first complete German translation by the Austrian orientalist and diplomat Joseph von Hammer-Purgstall in June 1814.[2] His response was immediately enthusiastic. He felt a deep emotional and artistic kinship with the exuberant songfulness of the medieval Persian poet, and immediately sat down to write a poem in his style. The encounter with Hafez' poetry marked the onset of a period of renewed poetic vitality in Goethe's creative life, unparalleled since his youth, that would give rise to his own "Divan."

This poetic rejuvenation coincided with Goethe's trips in the summer months of 1814 and 1815 to his home region, the area near the confluence of the Rhine and Main rivers in the western part of Germany. He wrote the earliest poems of the cycle while travelling by stagecoach from Weimar to Wiesbaden with Hafez' Diwan in his pocket. They form a kind of poetic trip diary that projects a dual motion connecting the actual westward travel impressions to a fictional journey eastward to the Orient. Upon his arrival, Goethe had composed a total of 30 poems. The first edition of the *West-East Divan*, published in 1819, would include over 200 poems of various lengths, followed by an extended commentary.

Goethe had good reasons to want to escape from the world surrounding him into a distant, idealised realm. He felt an urge to flee from the wreckage and turmoil of the Napoleonic wars and the subsequent liberation wars. He needed to break away from the hypernationalistic and hyperreligious cultural climate of the post-Napoleonic years. He wanted to distance himself from the pressure placed on him by many of his contemporaries to acclaim his liberated German fatherland with politically engaged, patriotic poetry. And, in a gesture of self-centred withdrawal repeated at other painful junctures of his life, he may also have wanted to avoid the daily sight of his wife Christiane's worsening health.

In the encounter with Hafez, he found a poetic summons, a welcome invitation of release from all those strictures. He found a refuge in an alternate reality, an imaginary realm of peace, love and pleasure far removed from the current impediments to his creativity. In the life of the founder of Islam, Muhammad, he found a name for his withdrawal and new beginning: "hegira," the French form of the Arabic "hijrah," denoting the flight of the prophet from Mecca to Medina in the year 622 that marked the beginning of the Islamic calendar. The reference to "hegira," used as a heading to the first poem of the collection, is repeated in his correspondence. His letter of 8 February 1815 to his friend Carl Ludwig von Knebel is explicit about the benefit of such an escape: "I bless my decision to undertake this hegira, for it has transported me away from the present time and from good old Middle Europe, which should be seen as a great boon from Heaven that does not befall everyone."

Goethe's cross-cultural voyage to the Orient parted company with the kind of approach to that region common among British and French statesmen and scholars of the 18th and 19th centuries, whom Edward Said would criticise in his path-breaking study *Orientalism*.[3] Rather than an exaggeration of the contrast between Orient and Occident in a so-called "clash of civilisations" and a style of discourse aimed at maintaining the colonial authority of the West over the Middle and Far East, Said found and affirmed in Goethe's approach an alternate discourse based on a dialogue with, rather than a Eurocentric representation of, the "Other." In response to the disapproval of his contemporaries for his fascination with the East, Goethe defended the mental versatility that enabled him to sway back and forth between the occidental and the oriental worlds:

Sinnig zwischen beyden Welten	'Twixt two worlds I love the way
Sich zu wiegen laß ich gelten,	Back and forth a man may sway;
Also zwischen Ost und westen	So between the East and West
Sich bewegen sey zum besten!	Moving to and fro's the best.

The intercultural openness pictured in the Weimar Hafez–Goethe monument is also represented on the original title page of Goethe's *West-East Divan*. Its dual-language design displays on the right the German title, publisher and date in Gothic and Roman letters; on the left, the Arabic calligraphy, surrounded by decorative ornamentation, reads: "The Eastern Divan of the Western Author" (see Figure 6).

This bilingual duality is continued in the Persian-German headings of the 11 chapters of the poem collection, from the initial "Moganni Nameh – Book of the Singer," to the final "Chuld Nameh – Book of Paradise."

The "singer" casts himself as a travelling merchant who rides with his caravan through a landscape of sandy desert expanses and oases, moving under the starry sky between far-away cities along ancient trade routes. Linked by commercial exchanges and cultural bonds, the landscape and people of the Orient are sketched in broad brushstrokes, forming a peaceful counterpoint to the European battlefields of Goethe's time. To be a nomad, to stay in motion, is the poet-trader's calling. His mobile lifestyle embraces a philosophy that opens him up to change and to meeting the unknown, while staying faithful to his chosen path. His journey is not only an occupation; it is the symbolic essence of life, for which the open-ended, spare landforms of the Middle East offer a well-suited backdrop. In an emphatic defence of both his nomadic lifestyle and mental mobility, the poet begs:

Freysinn	*Free thought*
Laßt mich nur auf meinem Sattel gelten!	Just let me have my saddle!
Bleibt in euren Hütten, euren Zelten!	You can remain in your huts, your tents,
Und ich reite froh in alle Ferne,	And I shall ride joyously into the distance,
Über meiner Mütze nur die Sterne.	Above my cap only the stars.

During his journey, the poet stands in constant communication with his counterpart Hafez, invoking him as his companion, his "twin brother" and the model of his artistic creativity. Hafez' songwriting offers him an example of non-Greek, non-classical verse-making, whose fluidity he likens to the flow of the Euphrates River. The alliance with Hafez is reasserted repeatedly, in a common enmity to the "monks" and clerics, the rule-makers and dogmatists. It is a psychological and literary bond that reaches across historical, spatial and cultural boundaries. As was the case with Hafez, the "memoriser" of the Koran, whose songs reached beyond the confines of religious teachings, Goethe's poetry wanders into the free space existing beyond laws. It is a figurative space that embraces cosmic and terrestrial realms in its ability to express both the joy of the moment and the awe of eternity.

In the wide expanses of Hafez' oriental world, the poet recognises and reasserts his own dual poetic and scientific calling. He must stay attuned to the "all-life" of nature in order to celebrate the connected action of the elements.

In the hot climate of the South, the sand – "dust" – is the primordial element. Powered by the warm winds, the dust can marry with the wet stormy air to transform the desert into moist plant life, where everything suddenly sprouts and greens. Its counterpart is the wintry wind from the North, whose icy breath torments and freezes all living creatures. Just as it had the power to defeat the mighty army of the Mongolian ruler Tamerlane, Hafez' contemporary, the icy winter wind triumphed over Napoleon's "grande armée" in Goethe's own times. "The Winter and Timur" shows more clearly than any other poem of the *West-East Divan* how the mirror image of oriental poetry aids the poet not only to escape, but to transpose, dramatise and intensify contemporary reality.

"Suleika Nameh – The Book of Zuleika" is the best-known and longest part of the *West-East Divan.* In 1869, Herman Grimm disclosed that a real love story – Goethe's relationship with Marianne von Willemer, formed during his 1814 and 1815 summer stays at the Willemer residence, the "Gerbermühle," near Frankfurt – was the biographical background for the poetic dialogue between the older poet Hatem and his beloved Zuleika. After Herman Grimm had documented that Marianne von Willemer was the actual author of several of the poems incorporated in the book, critics were long fixated on investigating or second-guessing the lived experience hidden behind its poetic language. More recently, attention has shifted toward recognising how much of the lovers' poetic duet was shaped by the literary codes of oriental love poetry, from which it borrowed its tropes, dual imagery and symbolism: moon and sun, rose and nightingale, curling hair and snakes, pearls and songs. Space returns here to become a central theme of the book, but physical distance becomes a subjective notion, diminished or heightened by the mood of the lover. The lover-wanderer seeks to gather all the treasures of the Orient, from Hindustan to the Red Sea, to bring them to his beloved. His heart can race in hyperbolic flights across space to meet his kindred soul. Elsewhere, he uses the power of his song to eliminate distance magically. The manifold messages exchanged by the lovers – wind, bird songs, eye signals, poem lines from Hafez' "ghazals" – combine and fuse artificial and experiential codes in an intricate web of exchanges that transcend distance and separation.

A well-known symbol of the lovers' secret code is Goethe's poem about the fan-shaped leaf of the Gingko biloba, one of the oldest trees on earth, originally grown in China and Japan and imported to Europe in the 18th century. In three short stanzas, the poet-scientist-lover reflects on the multiple meanings of the leaf's dual shape. Its interplay of unity and duality speaks of the deep interconnectedness of the lovers, but it can also allude to the overarching concept of unity and duality in Goethe's philosophy of nature, or to the hybridity of poetic language.

Gingo biloba

Dieses Baum's Blatt, der von Osten
Meinem Garten anvertraut,

Gingko biloba

Here's a leaf the East, with favour,
To my garden would confide –

Gibt geheimen Sinn zu kosten,	With secret meaning we may savour,
Wie's den Wissenden erbaut.	To the wise a vital guide.
Ist es Ein lebendig Wesen?	Do we view one living being
Das sich in sich selbst getrennt,	That has split itself in two?
Sind es zwey? die sich erlesen,	Did two things find each other
Daß man sie als Eines kennt.	To offer a united view?
Solche Frage zu erwiedern	To give an answer to this query
Fand ich wohl den rechten Sinn;	I have found the right reply:
Fühlst du nicht an meinen Liedern	Won't my singing give the feeling
Daß ich Einst und doppelt bin.	That both two and one am I?

"Saki Nameh – The Cup-Bearer's Book" engages the reader in a taboo-breaking cultural expedition. Its locale is a wine tavern, in Hafez' day often a house of ill repute, where the poet Hatem enjoys drinking wine to his heart's content, served by the handsome cup-bearer Saki, just as his "alter ego" Hafez did, notorious for his drinking and bisexual inclinations. While "The Cup-Bearer's

Book" openly champions Hafez' defiance of the Muslim prohibition against wine-drinking by extolling the mind-expanding and creative virtues of inebriety, the Western author can hide behind Hafez' promiscuous lifestyle to challenge the cultural taboo of his own time against same-sex relationships. The latter challenge is more difficult to carry out than the former, and involves a subtle role-switching game. While it is the young Saki who is cast into the role of the seducer, eager to be kissed and fondled and jealous of his female counterpart Zuleika, the older poet plays the part of the pedagogue eager to expand his pupil's philosophical education by inviting him to contemplate God's presence in the universe. Past and present, religious and sexual taboo-breaking meet in a common rejection of stifling orthodox prescriptions.

The introductory poem "Hegira" had not only prefigured Hatem's visit to Hafez' site of sensual pleasures; it had also announced his final journey into the afterlife. "Chuld Nameh – The Book of Paradise" was composed in several writing stages that extended beyond the first *Divan* publication. It includes poetic samples that were not derived from Hafez but freely extrapolated from the Koran and other Islamic sources. Projected through the lens of the Western author, its ironic portrayal borders on the blasphemous. In accordance with Muhammad's promise to the fallen heroes of the battle of Badr, the poet is greeted at the gate of paradise by a heavenly virgin, one of the beautiful houris dedicated to the faithful. The poet is convinced he has found his beloved Zuleika again. Men are the only humans entitled to the heavenly realm, with the exception of the four virtuous women: the Prophet Muhammad's wife, his daughter Fatima, Zuleika, and the Virgin Mary, mother of Jesus. Four faithful animals – a donkey, a wolf, a small dog and a cat – are also allowed access to paradise. The poet is not only fascinated by his houri's resemblance to Zuleika, but is particularly impressed when hearing that she speaks in German pair rhymes! The book's humour is aimed at the male-centredness of the depiction of eternal life and its fixation on the continuation of individuality into eternity, until all the irony dissipates in the transition from sensory apprehension to transcendent diffusion of the self in the universe and the transformation of individual love into cosmic love that anticipates the final mystical vision of Goethe's *Faust* drama.

Goethe's acquaintance with the poetry of Hafez not only ushered in a phase of poetic self-revitalisation; it also took him on an extended vicarious journey: a four-year-long imaginary voyage to the Orient that demanded a shift of psychological focus from Europe to Persia, and total mental immersion in a new cultural environment. He wrote to Christian Heinrich Schlosser in a letter of 23 January 1815 that Shiraz – the southern provincial capital, birthplace of his "twin brother" Hafez and an oasis city still praised today for its gardens, flowers and grapes as well as its literary heritage – had become the "centre" of his poetic world "from which I extend my excursions... in all directions." With a nod to the warm season, a letter from Wiesbaden to Christiane on 4 June 1815 summoned the same mental translocation: "Roses are blossoming to the fullest, nightingales are singing to one's wishes and it does not take an effort to transpose one's self to Shiraz."

In the years following his all-absorbing identification with Hafez, the stationary traveller dedicated himself single-mindedly to the study of oriental literature, reading Persian, Turkish and Arabic fiction in translations by his contemporaries Joseph von Hammer-Purgstall[4] and the Prussian diplomat and orientalist Heinrich Friedrich von Diez[5] (who disagreed vehemently with his colleague's translations). At the same time, he expanded his literary survey with a systematic study of the history of the region, new Koran editions and biographies of Muhammad, along with forays into the pre-Islamic, Zoroastrian nature cult of the Parsi. Between 1815 and 1818, Goethe also consulted an impressive array of travel accounts: past and contemporary reports of travellers through the entire Asian continent from the Ottoman Empire all the way to Ceylon and China.[6] Travel narratives are the "best tools" to update one's knowledge of a region, his notes pointed out. Stopping short of actually learning Arabic, he spent a good deal of time familiarising himself with Arabic and Persian calligraphy with the help of the Heidelberg orientalist Heinrich Eberhard Gottlob Paulus and the Jena scholar Johann Gottfried Ludwig Kosegarten. Pages of those writing exercises have survived. His *Tag- und Jahres-Hefte zu 1818* (*Annals for 1818*) tell us that all this reading, excerpting and writing activity was aimed at one single objective: "to feel increasingly at home" in the Orient.

What does Goethe's years-long, intensive work of cross-cultural immersion tell us about the mindset of the author?

Not only are we faced with an effort to escape or to break loose from the confines of the surrounding culture, but we encounter an amazing example of intercultural openness, a boundless curiosity for exploring the unknown and a reverence for cultural diversity, coupled with a readiness for self-transformation. The journey of discovery of "the other" is a transformative experience, a training ground for self-metamorphosis. In order to gain an appreciation for the literary production of the Orient, "we must orientalise ourselves," his notes observed. We must be willing to overcome the narrow boundaries of nationalism and Eurocentrism in order to reinvent ourselves. The last stanza of the famous poem "Selige Sehnsucht" ("Blessed Longing") could also apply to the experience of being born again through intercultural discovery:

Und so lang du das nicht hast,	And until you gain the best,
Dieses: stirb und werde!	This: die and become!
Bist du nur ein trüber Gast	You are but a doleful guest,
Auf der dunklen Erde.	On an earth that's dark and glum.

Judging that his audience was not as receptive to the challenge as he may have wished, Goethe added a lengthy explanatory supplement to his poetic collection prior to its initial publication, "Notes and Essays for a Better Understanding of the *West-East Divan*," with copious historical and literary annotations. One of the essays,

"Neuere, Neueste" ("Newer, Newest Thoughts"), includes a translated text by the 19th-century Persian diplomat Mirza Aboul Hassan Khan, which Goethe excerpts from its French translation:

> A king who stifles trade closes the doors of well-being in the face of his army. What judicious man would wish to visit a country with that kind of reputation? If you want to earn a good name, you should treat merchants and envoys with respect. Those who are great will treat travellers well, to gain a good name. The country that does not protect foreigners will soon perish. Be a friend to strangers and travellers, for they are a means for acquiring a good reputation. Be hospitable, appreciate those passing through, beware of being unjust to them. Whoever follows this advice of the envoy will surely benefit from it.

Along with the West–East invitation to intercultural discovery as a means of psychological renewal at the individual level, diplomat Mirza Aboul Hassan Khan's message of advice and warning to governments at the collective level, which Goethe transmitted to his own compatriots, has an echo that resonates with undiminished energy and urgency across the ages.

To Latin America with Alexander von Humboldt

Goethe's scientific interaction with the explorer and polymath Alexander von Humboldt spans more than three decades. It peaked in 1813 with the publication of his pictorial representation of Humboldt's topography of South America, *Höhen der alten und neuen Welt bildlich verglichen* (*Comparative Heights of the Old and the New World*).

Goethe met Alexander von Humboldt in the 1790s while the young Prussian mine inspector was visiting his older brother Wilhelm in Jena near Weimar, where Goethe frequently spent time with scientists at the university and with his literary collaborator Friedrich Schiller. The nineties marked a period of more intensive occupation with science for Goethe, following the first publication in 1790 of his treatise on the metamorphosis of plants, *Die Metamorphose der Pflanzen*. Although Alexander von Humboldt was much more devoted to mathematical precision than Goethe, they both shared a boundless curiosity for a variety of scientific fields, including botany, physiology and geology. Both were motivated by an interest in the theory of the "formative drive" developed by Johann Friedrich Blumenbach, the Göttingen specialist whose investigations in comparative anatomy had marked a turning point in the natural sciences, moving the study of organic life away from mechanical models. Unlike inanimate matter, Blumenbach postulated, plant, animal and human organisms each possessed their own intrinsic laws of development. Alexander von Humboldt also brought to Jena his new fascination for animal electricity or galvanism. Side by side with Goethe, he engaged in experiments in search of the secret of the "life force" animating organisms. While Humboldt's extended stay in Jena in the spring of 1797 would remain the period of his closest scientific collaboration with Goethe, his impact was a lifelong one.

After the death of his mother, Alexander von Humboldt inherited enough wealth to be able to realise his youthful dream of travelling around the world. In this age of global naval expansion, the quest for new maritime trade routes went hand in hand with scientific discovery, creating opportunities for young adventurers and scientists to explore new lands in search of mineral and vegetal riches. Humboldt's dream of global circumnavigation had also been stimulated by his friendship with Georg Forster, who had accompanied his father Johann Reinhold Forster on Captain Cook's second South Seas voyage and returned to write his *A Voyage Round the World* in 1777, soon translated into German as *Reise um die Welt während der Jahre 1772 bis 1775*.[1] Forster's best-selling narrative was another of Humboldt's and Goethe's shared passions.

Humboldt left Germany in April 1798 for Paris with the hope of joining a seafaring expedition. He purchased the newest scientific instruments and secured the collaboration of the like-minded French botanist Aimé Bonpland. As Napoleon's wars made sea travel from France increasingly risky, the two young scientists went to Madrid to petition the Spanish king, Carlos IV, for permission to visit the Spanish colonies of Central and South America. The passports they received opened the door for the five-year-long journey that took them on 5 June 1799 from La Coruña on the Atlantic coast of Spain to what is now Venezuela, Columbia, Ecuador, Peru, Mexico and Cuba. The expedition was capped by a visit to President Jefferson in the new United States of America. Humboldt and Bonpland would not return to Bordeaux, France until 1 August 1804.

During the hazardous travel across oceans, rivers, virgin forests and high Andean paths, transatlantic correspondence was a sporadic, one-way effort, and the safe arrival of letters was uncertain. Nevertheless, Humboldt used every opportunity to dispatch numerous letters to France and Germany, eager to publicise the highlights of his journey to his scientific colleagues, his brother and friends. From Paris, translated excerpts were printed in Weimar through the auspices of the publisher Friedrich Justin Bertuch, whose monthly journal, the *Allgemeine Geographische Ephemeriden* (*General Geographic Ephemerides*), specialised in world geography, discovery and maps of remote areas of the globe. With a modern business flair for the role of publicity in catching readers' attention, Bertuch nourished the curiosity of his provincial German public with exciting sea travel adventures and discoveries. As a reader of the *General Geographic Ephemerides,* Goethe had access to over a dozen letters and reports about Humboldt's journey during his absence.

"My life here is wonderful," the excited young traveller exclaimed in a letter written in Cumaná (today Venezuela) on 15 November 1800 and published in an April 1802 report, "Everything around me is new, grand and majestic." In another *Ephemerides* report, also published in April 1802, Humboldt compared the shapes of the South American and African coastlines and theorised that the two land masses must have been joined in a distant past prior to the emergence of plants and animals, a startlingly astute observation more than a century before the theory of continental drift and plate tectonics would be articulated. A May 1802 account broke the news that Alexander von Humboldt had reached the Casiquiare, the famed natural canal connecting the Orinoco River in the north to tributaries of the Amazon in the south, and that he had been able to map "the intricate parallelogram, where the water flows from four opposite sides in opposite directions." The August 1803 issue brought a letter from Lima, Peru announcing that on 23 June 1802 Humboldt and his companions had almost reached the top of the Chimborazo volcano south of Quito, which, at 6,310 metres above sea level, was at the time believed to be the highest mountain on earth. Their ascension had become increasingly difficult, the report added, as they struggled with altitude sickness and icy footholds, but they continued climbing until a deep, wide chasm blocked them from reaching the summit. Nonetheless, the letter concluded that Humboldt used his instruments to measure their highest attained altitude of 5,878 metres.

This spectacular news was followed by an unconfirmed rumour that "the famous traveller had died of yellow fever in Acapulco." Had the German scientist met the same fatal journey's end as La Pérouse and countless other vanished voyagers? The sad rumour was immediately refuted by an announcement from Wilhelm von Humboldt that his brother had just departed from Charleston on the Atlantic coast and was on his way back to Paris. "We can only hope soon to be able to confirm this news," the *Ephemerides* publisher chimed in, knowing how to hold his readers in suspense. Such a death and resurrection tale only heightened the mythical stature of the transatlantic traveller. Humboldt's confirmed arrival in Paris was greeted by Goethe in his 30 July 1804 letter to Wilhelm with the joyous remark that, "for us," he is "rising again from the dead!"

There was a long hiatus between Alexander von Humboldt's and Aimé Bonpland's return and the publication of the scientific results of their journey to the New World. The project, divided by discipline, would mushroom into a multi-volume, two-decades-long undertaking. During that time, Bertuch's *Ephemerides* continued to perform its promotional role as Humboldt's prime press organ and mediator with the German reading public. In April and May 1805, Bertuch's journal was the first to publish in German translation the recapitulation of Humboldt's travels compiled by his Parisian friend Jean-Claude Delamétherie. Based on the explorer's lectures to the

Académie des Sciences in Paris, *J. C. Delamétherie's vorläufige Nachricht von der durch die Herren v. Humboldt und Bonpland in den Jahren 1799, 1800, 1801, 1802, 1803 und 1804 nach den Wendekreisen unternommenen Reise* (*J. C. Delamétherie's Preliminary Report on a Voyage to the Tropics Undertaken by the Gentlemen von Humboldt and Bonpland in the Years 1799, 1800, 1801, 1802, 1803 and 1804*) summarised the successive stations of the Humboldt-Bonpland expedition: crossing the great plains, the Llanos, south of Caracas; a 500-mile-long round-trip journey by boat on the mosquito- and crocodile-infested Orinoco River to the Casiquiare and Rio Negro connection with the Amazon; an intermission on the island of Cuba; a boat trip on the Magdalena River to Bogotá and a visit to the botanical collection of the Spanish scientist José Celestino Mutis there; a trek on muleback across the Andes to Quito; foiled plans to connect with Captain Nicolas Baudin's circumnavigation of the globe; the ascent and exploration of the multiple volcanoes around Quito; Humboldt's discovery of the magnetic equator on his second cross-Andean journey to Lima; a sea journey from Guayaquil to Acapulco followed by a sojourn in Mexico City, the capital of New Spain, and multiple excursions to the surrounding volcanoes; a second trip to Cuba; and finally a visit to Philadelphia and Washington.

After Humboldt's return to Europe, the vagaries of the Napoleonic wars brought him, in late 1805, back to his Berlin home grounds, where he focused on publicising some of his travel observations and research results. In February 1806, Goethe received his first post-America letter from Humboldt, who invited him to venture out "in a harsh winter night" for a stroll under "the beautiful canopy of the tropical forests" with the help of his enclosed lecture *Ideen zu einer Physiognomik der Gewächse* (*Ideas on the Physiognomy of Plants*), which he had just presented to the Berlin Academy. Humboldt made a point of connecting his tantalising vegetal depictions with Goethe's own morphological and holistic approach, which explained plant growth as the progressive mutation of the leaf organ. In beautifully crafted, lively prose, his text detailed the visual characteristics of 19 plant types, which were grouped into aesthetic categories rather than dry, taxonomic classifications. The same letter disclosed that his forthcoming treatise on the geography of plants would include an illustrated dedication to Goethe, who returned the favour by immediately issuing an announcement of Humboldt's work accompanied by enticing samples of his plant descriptions, such as the palm, banana, cactus, aloe and orchid forms. His review of the piece was included in the 14 March 1806 issue of the most prominent periodical published under his patronage, the *Jenaische Allgemeine Literaturzeitung* (*Jena General Literary Magazine*).

Goethe's promotion of Humboldt's essay was characteristic of his strategy of selective alliance. After enthusiastically immersing himself in the tropical vegetation conjured up by his correspondent, he only allied publicly with those aspects of the emerging Humboldtian science that were germane to his own highly visual and aesthetic approach to science, as exemplified in his *Metamorphosis of Plants*. In a similar manner, it was also Goethe who would suggest a formal separation between the literary part of the *Ansichten der Natur* (*Views of Nature*), in which Humboldt's essay on the physiognomy of plants was later included, and its strictly scientific commentary that included copious amounts of numerical data.

"When a friend with whom we agree on the main points of our thinking tells us about the world and its various parts, it is almost the same as if we had seen them ourselves." Goethe's avowal on 15 September 1800 of his visual identification with the description of the Montserrat mountain and abbey that Wilhelm von Humboldt had sent him from Barcelona, Spain one year after Alexander's visit there, also applies to his total response to Humboldt's *Ideen zu einer Geographie der Pflanzen* (*Essay on the Geography of Plants*). Just as was the case with the trip to Montserrat, the homebound traveller was able by sheer force of the mind's eye to turn his armchair journey to the tropics into a substitute for actual travel.

The long-awaited German version of Humboldt's book arrived in Weimar on 16 March 1807. It was decorated with an allegorical frontispiece by the artist Bertel Thorvaldsen showing the naked god of poetry, Apollo, unveiling a multi-breasted statue of the goddess of nature. A tablet at her feet with the inscription *Metamorphosis of Plants* was underwritten with the name of its author "Göthe." We know from multiple sources how delighted and flattered Goethe was with Humboldt's recognition, which put on display the symbiosis between art and science that Goethe achieved in his poetry.

In the following days, from 17 to 20 March 1807,

Goethe read and re-read Humboldt's work, yet he found frustrating the unexplained absence of a geographic chart referenced by the author. He made up for the missing illustration by sketching a pictorial representation of the equatorial environment described by the explorer. The "imaginary landscape" that he drew was coloured by his artistic collaborator Johann Heinrich Meyer, and would also serve as a visual aid for his weekly lecture to a small group of Weimar ladies. His notes indicate that the subject matter on 1 April 1807 was dedicated to the comparative geology of the New and the Old Worlds. Prior to the meeting, Goethe also reached back to the *General Geographic Ephemerides* in order to recapture the highlights of Humboldt's journey in his pencil drawing, which he titled *Höhen der alten und neuen Welt bildlich verglichen* (*Comparative Heights of the Old and the New World*). Lacking Humboldt's illustration, his own visual representation was an indispensable means of showing his audience the vast difference in proportion between the European Alps and the American Andes. Next to its immediate didactic purpose, his image also had an aesthetic goal. In a pictorial interpretation of the missing plate, which Humboldt had called "Naturgemälde der Tropenländer" ("Picture of Nature in the Tropical Countries"), Goethe's imaginary landscape interpreted it as a painting in neo-classical style.

There appear to have been three stages in Goethe's involvement with Humboldt's work that we find replicated elsewhere in his creative process: intensive absorption, then mental appropriation of his model, followed by its systematic intermedial transformation. As shown in Figure

7, the third step transformed the original essay with its wealth of empirical data into a holistic visual composition by juxtaposing altitude and vegetation zones of the "New" with the "Old" world inside a single pictorial frame. The vertical reference points integrated Humboldt's precise measurements, but reduced numbers and names to a minimum, discreetly inserted into the right- and left-hand borders of the picture. On the right-hand side, the four Andean volcanoes – Chimborazo, Antisana, Cotopaxi and Tungurahua – their cliff faces bathed in bright light, are placed above the 5,000-metre line in decreasing order of height; opposite them on the left side, the three Alpine peaks – Mont Blanc, Schreckhorn and Wetterhorn, as well as the Sicilian volcano Monte Etna – are pictured below the 5,000-metre line in descending order of elevation. The precise information in Humboldt's geographic essay gives way to the global aesthetic effect induced by the vegetal physiognomy. Green colour masses stand for vegetation zones, while the difference between the climates of the temperate and the tropical hemispheres is demonstrated by the contrast between illuminated and shaded halves of the picture. The horizontal colour gradation from green to white and blue translates the zonal thesis of Humboldt's essay into visual language – his thesis being namely that the growth of vegetation reaches 2,200 metres higher in the equinoctial zones of South America than in the temperate zones of Europe, with the breadth of the snow region being twice as thin in the Andes as in the Alps. The farm hut, or "Viehmeierei," below the summit of the Antisana volcano, mentioned several times by Humboldt to indicate that in the zone near the equator human settlements can extend above 4,000 metres, is placed directly across from the summit of the Schreckhorn on the left side. Below, to illustrate the height of the high plateaus of the Americas, the Peruvian town of Micui-pampa is juxtaposed with the top of the Etna, while Quito and Mexico City face the Gotthard summit and hospice. From the point of view of Goethe, the traveller to Switzerland and Italy, the European elevations were dwarfed by the fantastic heights reached by the South American explorer.

Not all tree shapes blend into green colour masses. Goethe's composition reserved a special place for a botanical specimen that Humboldt had singled out as a striking expression of the vitality of plant life in the tropics: the wax palm tree of the Andes or *Ceroxylon andicola*, today the national tree of Columbia, which grows at altitudes of 1,800 to 2,800 metres. To draw attention to a phenomenon demonstrating the close interaction between plant life and climate, Goethe placed the Andean palm tree on top of a mountain ridge across from the snow line and the barren Gotthard summit on the left side of the picture.

There are also contemporary icons embedded in the symbolic design of the landscape. These easily identifiable signs hark back in ironic jest to the salient points of Humboldt's essay. The small balloon above the highest summit of the American Cordilleras represents the feat of Humboldt's friend, the French chemist Louis Joseph Gay-Lussac, who became the highest man on earth on 16 September 1804, when his hot-air balloon reached an altitude of 7,016 metres above sea level. Underneath the balloon icon, just below the summit of the Chimborazo, the tiny figure of the second highest man on earth, Alexander von Humboldt, can be seen waving to the diminutive shape of Horace Bénédict de Saussure standing slantways below him on top of Mont Blanc. The only element at odds with the peacefulness of the idyllic scenery is a monstrous crocodile head emerging from the river in the bottom right hand of the picture, whose open jaw embodies the threats hidden in the deceivingly placid environment.

Goethe's illustration of the contrast between the Southern and Northern Hemispheres not only provides a compelling example of his eidetic gift of visualisation. It also impresses us, creatures of the age of digital imaging, through its symbolic mode of representation. By freely combining several pictorial devices and manipulating image outline, size and spatial disposition, he was able to reduce drastically the need for textual information. His imaginary landscape worked in many ways like a model for digital imaging by transforming scientific discourse into a visual language of spatial relations and colour symbolism that appealed to sensory perception as a window on cognitive information processing.

Goethe sent a copy of his picture to Humboldt, asking him for his comments and corrections. There was no apparent response from Humboldt, giving rise to speculation about the cause of his silence, but a month later the German version of the missing "tableau physique des régions équinoxiales" ("Physical View of Equatorial Regions"), originally folded inside the French version of Humboldt's geographic essay, arrived in Weimar.

The design of the plate illustrates a striking divergence between Humboldt's and Goethe's approaches to the visualisation of science (see Figure 8). As Humboldt's overall goal was exactitude and comprehensiveness of information, his "tableau" combines both tabular and pictorial elements inside a single frame. In contrast to Goethe's economy of textual information for the sake of aesthetic holism, the word-image proportion is reversed in Humboldt's intricate illustration of the interaction of plants with their environment. The central, bipartite mountain panel is flanked on each side by columns of numbers and words that occupy half of the total plate. The left side of the dome-shaped Chimborazo displays the visible features of the volcanic region, while its right side consists of a cross-section diagram inside which a total of 250 plant names are arranged according to their altitudinal distribution. The informational columns on each side of the central panel list the abiotic factors – altitudinal, meteorological, chemical and physical – that altogether combine to affect biological life. The hybrid mode of representation with its mix of image and words disrupts the organic harmony of the composition, but it focuses the viewer's attention on the explicative purpose of the design meant to point to the invisible factors that determine the emergence of the organic forms. Since nothing in nature exists in isolation, Humboldt considered the inclusion of those multivariate factors in his ecosystem of the Chimborazo to be crucial to making explicit the connectivity of plant life to its environment. Such ecological interplay remained implicit in Goethe's strictly pictorial mode of representation.

Goethe's comparative mountain view might have been forgotten without the active engagement of the publisher Bertuch and his *General Geographic Ephemerides*. Recognising the role of illustrations in the dissemination of geographic knowledge, and having already invested considerable effort in the promotion of Humboldt's journey, Bertuch sought Goethe's collaboration in preparing a printable version of his neo-classical landscape. In early 1813, an etching based on the original design was executed by the engraver Johann Christian Starcke and corrected by Goethe (see Figure 9).

The etching was so successful that Bertuch had it reissued as a separate offprint in black-and-white and coloured versions. Soon after, the General Direction of Press and Publishing in Paris asked for permission to publish its own copy with minor adaptations for the French public.

From Paris, where he was again residing, Humboldt participated in the undertaking. The illustrated outcome was published with a reference to Goethe's artistic role as *Esquisse des Principales Hauteurs des deux continens [sic]* (*Sketch of the Principal Heights of the Two Continents*). A number of copies and imitations of the French version appeared in France and Great Britain. They soon began to incorporate the outlines of the Himalayan mountain range and to find their way into geographical atlases. Although Alexander von Humboldt is credited with having inspired the comparative geographic chart genre, the intermedial creativity of the armchair traveller Goethe played a decisive part in creating the "comparative view" of mountains that became a new tool of geographic popularisation.

Undeniably, Humboldt's dedication of his *Geography of Plants* to the author of *Metamorphosis of Plants* and Goethe's counter-dedication of his *Comparative Heights of the Old and the New World* to Humboldt marked the high point of their public association, an alliance that was rooted in their common fascination for the dynamism of plant organisms and their sensual pleasure in the visual beauty of the green world. Published in the aftermath of his involvement with Humboldt's botanical treatise, the second part of Goethe's novel *Die Wahlverwandtschaften* (*Elective Affinities*) would include in the diary of his house- and garden-loving Ottilie the following summative tribute to the explorer:

> Only that natural scientist is worthy of our respect who can depict and portray the most alien and strangest things in their own locale and its surroundings, always in their own element. How I should like just once to hear Humboldt speak.

To apprehend, study and show the interaction of alien life forms with their specific environment was indeed Humboldt's most influential feat, for which he is still revered and known as the founding father of ecology today.

Goethe and Humboldt met only infrequently after the explorer's return from his South American expedition and just 22 letters – presumably a fraction of their total correspondence – have survived.[2] But from Paris, where he lived between 1808 and 1827, Humboldt continued to send copies of his major works to Weimar: the lavishly illustrated *Vues des Cordillères et Monumens [sic] des Peuples indigènes de l'Amérique*[3] (*Views of the Cordilleras and Monuments of the Indigenous Peoples of the Americas*) in 1810, later followed by the successive instalments of his multipartite *Relation historique du Voyage aux régions équinoxiales du Nouveau Continent*[4] (*Personal Narrative of Travel to the Equinoctial Regions of the New Continent*) and his most important essays. Each arrival of a new publication prompted an intensive reading experience, the traces of which are left in Goethe's diaries and correspondence. During each new immersion, time became a meaningless lapse as Humboldt's worldwide vision had the power to erase space and time in the act of imagination. Humboldt's mental versatility never ceased to astound his friend. Paging through the *Essai politique sur l'île de Cuba*[5] (*Political Essay on the Island of Cuba*) in February 1827, Goethe came across, to his amazement, Humboldt's idea of a canal that would connect the Atlantic and Pacific oceans across the Isthmus of Panama. In a conversation recorded by Johann Peter Eckermann on 21 February 1827, Goethe confided that he would like "to hold on to life some extra fifty years" just to be able to see such an undertaking realised. In 1831, not long before his death, Goethe was able to read Humboldt's *Fragmens [sic] de géologie et de climatologie asiatiques*[6] (*Fragments on Asian Geology and Climatology*) in order to partake mentally in his friend's last long journey abroad, to Russia and Central Asia.

Goethe's reception of "Sur les lois que l'on observe dans la distribution des formes végétales"[7] ("On the Laws Dealing with the Distribution of Vegetal Forms"), which linked patterns of temperature to the emergence of specific plant forms around the earth, casts light on another side of his connection to Humboldt. His reaction to the piece indicates that partaking in Humboldt's view of nature as a global system with corresponding climate and vegetation zones across the continents held a therapeutic effect for him. The essay reached him just six days after the death of his life companion Christiane on 6 June 1816. Goethe responded to it with the poem "To Alexander von Humboldt," published in his collected works:

An Trauertagen	In days of mourning
Gelangte mir dein herrlich Heft!	Your superb essay reached me!
Es schien zu sagen:	It seemed to say:
Ermanne dich zu fröhlichem Geschäft!	Have courage and resume your work with cheer!
Die Welt in allen Zonen grünt und blüht	All regions of the world are greening and blooming
Nach ewigen beweglichen Gesetzen;	According to eternal motile laws;
Das wußtest du ja sonst zu schätzen,	That was something you once knew to value,
Erheitre so durch mich dein schwer bedrängt Gemüt!	Make use of me to lighten your anguished soul!

The same law that makes plants across the earth green and blossom, the poet asserts, the eternal dynamism that animates them, should also have a reanimating influence on him. Reminding his friend of their common belief in organic healing, stimulated by their earlier study of Blumenbach's physiology, he conjures up the power of internal regeneration to help alleviate the weight of mourning. Writing to his friend Sulpiz Boisserée on 24 June 1816, Goethe ascribes to the essay the soothing effect of "redirecting" him toward the "paths of nature" and "adorning the dark ground of the present moment with bright colourful pictures." Humboldt's demonstration of the constancy of vegetal renewal invited him to step out of his bleak mental enclosure to partake in its proven natural blessings.

If Goethe and Humboldt met and complemented each other in their approach to botany and their ecological instinct, they parted ways in their relationship to geology. At a time when the origin and history of the planet was a subject of intense debate, Alexander von Humboldt became a Plutonist, or Vulcanist, a vocal proponent of fire geology or the belief in the primary role played by explosions of the molten earth core in the formation of rocks and the upheaval of the earth's mountains. Instead, Goethe remained faithful to water geology or Neptunism, which posited a peaceful formation of rocks and mountains through the progressive sedimentation of a primeval ocean.

In March 1823, Goethe received a copy of Humboldt's *Ueber den Bau und die Wirkungsart der Vulcane in verschiedenen Erdstrichen*[8] (*On the Structure and the Influence of Volcanoes in Different Regions of the World*), which contradicted the Neptunist worldview that he had reasserted in the retrospective narration of his *Italian Journey.* The Humboldtian essay forcefully argued against the narrow geological knowledge of those who had witnessed only one eruption of an isolated volcano such as Vesuvius. The second part of Goethe's *Italian Journey* – which included accounts of his three ascents of Vesuvius on 2, 6 and 20 March 1787, where the dense clouds of steam and smoke prevented the prudent traveller from coming close to the crater – might have been a case in point. By contrast with most European travellers, whose exposure was limited to the volcanoes of Italy and Sicily, Humboldt underscored his own extensive study of the breadth and variety of volcanic activity in both hemispheres. Not only had he climbed to the edge of the crater of Mount Teide on the Canary Islands, he had observed at close range and measured the volcanic chasms above the Quito and Mexico plateaux. On the basis of his repeated direct exposure (as when, after lying on a ledge above the crater of the Pichincha on 26 and 28 May 1802, he reported in a published letter having been able to look down into the pitch-dark, fuming abyss that was large enough to contain entire mountains), he was able to point out that volcanoes were not an isolated physical occurrence of limited scope, but an interlinked system of underground channels and connections between a hot and molten inner core and the upper crust of the earth. The intimation to his implied reader was that no degree of mental intuition, no eidetic power of recollection or no imaginary voyage could ever claim to act as a substitute for the real observation and empirical study of the actual phenomenon. Goethe responded to

Humboldt's challenge by publicising his essay on volcanoes as an invitation from "a member of the old school" to study the new theory of the earth. The armchair traveller conceded that adopting Humboldt's Vulcanism and giving up his own preference for Neptunism would require an effort of real-life immersion in the fieldwork that was the basis of Humboldt's geological worldview "if his concrete reality were to become my reality." Rather than engaging in an open dispute with the Humboldtian science of the earth, Goethe preferred to channel the controversy into his own poetic work. In *Faust II*, the second part of his *Faust* drama, he has the Greek natural philosopher Thales, the proponent of the primeval action of water in the slow and peaceful sedimentation of rocks and mountains, engage in an argument with Anaxagoras, the advocate of their formation by violent, explosive upheaval. Elsewhere in *Faust II*, he even makes the satanic Mephisto function as a spokesman of Vulcanism.

While the debate concerning the geological formation of rocks has since reached a peaceful resolution, as the combined forces of heat, tectonic motion and sedimentation are now recognised to have played a role in the Earth's history, Goethe's fascination with the explorer Alexander von Humboldt and his passionate dedication to field study in several continents never ceased to provide a source of inspiration for his own global vision of nature.

Brazilian Treasures

Alexander von Humboldt's tropical expedition down the Orinoco River had ended at the junction between the Casiquiare canal and the Rio Negro, on the virtual line of demarcation between the Spanish and the Portuguese South American territories. Rather than dwelling on the century-old border dispute between the two rival colonies settled by the Treaty of Tordesillas, Humboldt focused on the topographic features that caused the natural canal to change its course near its border with Brazil.

Those hydraulic connections between north and south, the Orinoco and Amazon water systems, were where Goethe, upon receiving the second volume of Humboldt's *Relation historique* in 1821, rushed to join his friend in reliving one of the high points of his journey. From Weimar he writes back on 16 May 1821:

> I quickly opened the volume exactly in its middle and, with no hesitation at all, plunged alongside you into the wildest regions where mighty rivers do not simply flow unceasingly down their own courses, but try in a fashion long undiscovered to unite with each other.

At the same time as he was accompanying Humboldt on his geographic journey of discovery, the armchair traveller had already turned his sights toward the immense country stretching to the southwest of the line of demarcation. As a colony of the Portuguese crown closed off to the other European powers for several centuries, Brazil entered into world politics in 1808 when the Portuguese king, Joáo VI, and his entire court administration resettled from Lisbon to Rio de Janeiro to escape Napoleon's invasion of Portugal. The 2,000 newcomers, including administration and business people, transformed the country, opening it to global trade with friendly nations. In 1815, the Congress of Vienna declared the new political entity to be the United Kingdom of Portugal, Brazil and the Algarves; a few years later, the Empire of Brazil devolved from the bi-continental kingdom to become an independent country. Another milestone was marked in 1817, when the marital union of Leopoldina, daughter of the Habsburg Emperor Francis I, to the Brazilian heir Dom Pedro opened up Brazil to scientific exploration by a large team of Austrian and Bavarian naturalists who accompanied the Austrian princess on her bridal journey to her new home. Leopoldina, who helped inspire the scientific study of her new country, would also play a significant role in negotiating Brazil's independence from Portugal in 1822.

Goethe's interest in Brazil in the latter part of his life coincided to some extent with his official duties as a custodian of the Weimar duchy's collections. It was partly self-motivated, spurred by his curiosity for the immense, mysterious country that had just opened up to the outside world. He borrowed, purchased and read successively most of the contemporary travel accounts about Brazil, interacted with German travellers and explorers returning from the new country and negotiated the acquisition of samples of Brazilian flora and fauna for the renowned botanical garden of the Belvedere Palace in Weimar.

Not only did the encounter with Brazil reward Goethe's thirst for new geographic horizons, it also informed his ongoing studies in major scientific areas, including mineralogy and geology, as well as plant and animal morphology. In much less overt but no less intriguing ways, Goethe's vision of the Brazilian landscape – with its lush vegetation, its biological and ethnic diversity and the challenge of its slave-supported social structure – engaged his creative mind to the point of infiltrating the imaginary realm of the *Faust II* drama, his last poetic achievement.

Wilhelm Ludwig von Eschwege

The first Brazil experts with whom Goethe came in contact were mineralogists. In 1817, he read *A Treatise on Diamonds and Precious Stones* and *Travels in the Interior of Brazil, Particularly in the Gold and Diamond Districts of that Country*[1] by the British diamond dealer John Mawe, who had explored the mining region of Minas Gerais to assess the value of the gold and diamond industries for Brazil's economy. From Mawe's popular eyewitness accounts, backed by Robert Southey's voluminous *History of Brazil*, he learned about the "gold mountain" Itacolomi near Vila Rica, the present-day town of Ouro Preto. He read about the huge gold deposits mined there in the mid-18th century when the gold rush reached the peak of its attraction and about the continuous demand for more enslaved Africans to "wash" the gold and diamonds from the riverbeds of Minas Gerais. As a foreign observer, Mawe did not hold back his criticism of an economy entirely dependent on the toil and sweat of forced labour. In October 1817, Mawe was awarded membership of the Mineralogical Society of Jena through Goethe's auspices.

Also in 1817, the Weimar publisher Bertuch, who was always on the lookout for travel novelties, brought out the first Brazilian travelogue written by a German, Wilhelm Ludwig von Eschwege's *Journal von Brasilien, oder vermischte Nachrichten aus Brasilien*[2] (*Diary from Brazil, or Miscellaneous News from Brazil*), which Goethe immediately purchased and studied. Eschwege, a German mine prospector and engineer, had followed the Portuguese king to Brazil where he was appointed General Director of the Brazilian gold mines and acted as an early transcontinental liaison until he returned to Europe in 1821. His *Diary from Brazil* is a collection of miscellaneous texts that include descriptions of the iron works directed by Eschwege, economic statistics, discussions of Portuguese laws regarding the assimilation of Indians (the collective term preferred by indigenous Brazilians) and accounts about the native tribes of Minas Gerais – the Coroatos and the Puris – and the stigmatised "anthropophagous" nation of the Botocudos. Upon his return to Europe, Eschwege travelled to Weimar, where he married Sophie von Baumbach, a maid of honour to Grand Duchess Louise.

Eschwege's multiple visits to Goethe's house in 1822 and 1823 also cast light on the role played by Brazil as a supplier of precious stones to the European courts. Eschwege arrived in January 1822 with a set of diamonds that had piqued Grand Duke Carl August's interest. The Duke charged Goethe with conducting negotiations to purchase them, and a deal was concluded on 18 January. In November of the same year, Eschwege was back in Weimar with a larger assortment of 42 diamonds of different shapes and colours that he was eager to sell after failed negotiations in Vienna and Berlin. Goethe recommended acquisition of the entire collection to the Duke. A receipt for 715 Reichsthaler issued by Eschwege was signed by Goethe on behalf of Carl August on 28 December 1822, and the diamonds were included in the Duke's gem collection.

Scrutinising the precious stones raised questions about the process of crystallisation that shaped their structure. Goethe was helped in his inquiries by Eschwege's *Geognostisches Gemälde von Brasilien und wahrscheinliches Muttergestein der Diamanten*[3] (*Geological Tableau of Brazil and its Likely Bedrock of Diamonds*), a description of the geology of the granite and sandstone mountain ranges where gold, diamonds and other precious stones were found in the riverbeds around the peaks of Itacolomi and Itabirito. On 11 May 1822, right after it came off Bertuch's presses, Eschwege brought his small geological treatise to Goethe, who read it the same day. In Eschwege's depiction of Brazilian rock formations shaped by erosion Goethe must have found confirmation of his own preference for the Neptunist theory, popular since the late 18th century, that only the slow work of sedimentation and crystallisation, rather than violent volcanic action, caused rock formation. While that view may have explained the gold deposits in and around the mountains of the Brazilian interior, it could not account for the presence of hard diamonds, which can crystallise only at the high temperatures found deep in the Earth's mantle and therefore must have been propelled to the surface by volcanic eruptions. Carbon dating tells us today that a combination of Neptunist and volcanic dynamics must have been at work in forming the Brazilian sub-continent.

Maximilian zu Wied-Neuwied

The work of Prince Maximilian zu Wied-Neuwied, a former student of the Göttingen scientist Johann Friedrich Blumenbach and disciple of Alexander von Humboldt, helped reveal to the European public the beauty and the amazing ecological diversity of Brazil. Goethe had become acquainted with Wied-Neuwied through their mutual friend, botanist Nees von Esenbeck. Shortly after meeting Humboldt in Paris, Wied-Neuwied travelled to Brazil at his own expense, exploring the Atlantic coastal region between 4 August 1815 and 10 May 1817. His almost two-year-long trip took him up the eastern coast from Rio de Janeiro to Salvador and inside the Atlantic Forest, a vast region blessed with some of the richest biodiversity on the planet and home to several indigenous tribes. He returned to Germany with extensive field notes and drawings, a huge collection of plants, mammals, fish and birds and a native Indian companion who would serve him until his death.

Wied-Neuwied's expedition was discussed in Bertuch's *Ephemerides* and other widely read learned periodicals. His illustrated narrative *Reise nach Brasilien in den Jahren 1815 bis 1817*[4] (*Trip to Brazil in the Years 1815 to 1817*), published in two German volumes after his return, was received with great curiosity and translated into English and French. Goethe acquired the travelogue for his personal library and Bertuch displayed his own interest by issuing a bilingual, German-French edition of Wied-Neuwied's coloured plates of Brazilian animals, his *Abbildungen zur Naturgeschichte Brasiliens*[5] (*Illustrations Concerning the Natural History of Brazil*), followed by a sequence of four illustrated books on the natural history of Brazil. Wied-Neuwied's pictures of apes, reptiles and colourful birds arrested Goethe's attention, as his diary entry on the evening of 22 March 1821 attests: "I have been looking at Prince von Neuwied's birds and animals." Reflecting on the same pictures, his *Annals for 1821* ascribe to the astonishing novelty and artistic quality of Wied-Neuwied's illustrations the power of transcending distance and transporting him into another, far-away world.

Wied-Neuwied described the plants and animals of the tropical world with the keen eye of an artist. Stunned by the prodigality of the rainforest, where palm trees are interwoven with creeping plants and ferns and where colourful trumpet flowers hang from colossal trees, he repeatedly celebrated its intricate and multiform biodiversity. "The vegetation of this part of the Southern Hemisphere is so luxuriant," he marvelled in his travelogue, "that every lofty old tree becomes the emblem of a little world, a botanical garden of plants, truly rare, and certainly of an unknown kind."[6] As a specialist in zoology and ornithology, he was particularly curious about the many animal species in the Atlantic Forest. At every step he encountered an environment teeming with a multitude of wild animals, birds, snakes, amphibians and insects (see Figure 10). Nature's bounty seemed inexhaustible. The drawings singled out by Goethe aimed to document and illustrate the rich diversity of animal forms. Yet at the same time, Wied-Neuwied was also an enthusiastic hunter, shooting birds with abandon and proudly listing his prey, reliant as he was on the overabundance of wildlife not only to enrich his ornithological collection, but also to feed himself and his travelling companions. Two centuries later, the limits of nature's generosity have become painfully apparent in the Atlantic coastal region, where only a small fraction of the plant and animal species collected by the German explorer have survived the relentless deforestation and expansion of human activity in that most densely populated part of Brazil.

Although Wied-Neuwied frequently stopped along the coast to seek the hospitality of the sugar plantation owners whose hilltop mansions loomed above their slaves' huts, his travelogue refrains from commenting on Brazil's racial hierarchy. After all, his whole expedition, consisting of the two German naturalists Georg Wilhelm Freyreiss and Friedrich Sellow, ten local helpers and 16 mules, often depended on their hosts' generous services for their maintenance. Instead, the explorer's attention was focused on the Indian tribes of the Atlantic Forest. While Wied-Neuwied's ethnographic perspective remained thoroughly Eurocentric, he rejected prejudice and hearsay to seek direct encounters with the native Brazilians. The best example of the investigatory qualities for which his *Trip to Brazil* is still regarded as a pioneering document of comparative anthropology can be found in the chapter on the Botocudos, the fierce indigenous dwellers of the Atlantic Forest, long associated with European stereotypes of Brazilian cannibalism. It provides for the first time a nuanced portrayal of their social organisation, customs and family bonds, humanising a people previously caricatured for their "man-eating" propensities. Using his helper, the Botocudo Indian Quäck, as his instructor, Wied-Neuwied reduces the place and significance of cannibalism by contextualising it as an occasional ritual of revenge against defeated enemies or hostile settlers. Maximilian zu Wied-Neuwied's passion for the investigation of the life and culture of the American Indian nations later led him to undertake a trip to North America, west of the Missouri River, in the company of the Swiss painter Karl Bodmer. That new expedition took place between 1832 and 1834, after Goethe's death.

On his return from Brazil, Wied-Neuwied brought back a herbarium of 5,000 examples of over 1,000 plant species. He sought the help of the botanist Nees von Esenbeck in identifying them. In recognition of Goethe's path-breaking work in plant morphology, they decided to link a Brazilian *Malva* species to his name. The *Goethea* (*cauliflora or semperflorens*), a rare plant with bright red flowers emerging directly from the stem of lower-growing trees in the tropical forest, now ornaments many botanical gardens around the world. In its country of origin, the *Goethea* remains a tribute to Goethe's Brazilian interest. In his letter of 24 April 1823 to Nees von Esenbeck, Goethe, who was recovering from a life-threatening illness, conveyed his thanks to both naturalists for the naming of the *Goethea*, and expressed his special gratitude to the explorer of Brazil Prince Maximilian zu Wied-Neuwied, whom he would never meet in person, for one of his "most precious travel treasures."

Kaspar Maria von Sternberg

On his return voyage to Europe in July 1817, Wied-Neuwied crossed paths with the bridal ships bringing Leopoldina von Habsburg and the team of Austrian-Bavarian natural scientists to Brazil. The 11-man expedition included the Austrians Johann Christian Mikan, Johann Natterer and Johann Baptist Emanuel Pohl, together with their assistants and painters, and the Bavarians Johann Baptist von Spix and Carl Friedrich Philipp von Martius from Munich. Duke Carl August and Goethe, after unsuccessfully attempting to sponsor a scientist representing Prussia and Weimar, were most eager to acquire samples of the Brazilian findings. Goethe's correspondence with the scientific coordinator of the expedition, Carl Franz Anton von Schreibers, Director of the Viennese Museum of Natural History, documents these efforts.

But the scientist who played the most decisive role in helping Goethe interpret the flora and fauna of Brazil was the paleobotanist Kaspar Maria von Sternberg, who became one of Goethe's closest scientific colleagues during the last 12 years of his life. Initially, Sternberg had been selected to be the leader of Leopoldina's Brazilian expedition, a role that he had to decline for financial and health reasons, but he stayed in touch with the Austrian and Bavarian team members for years after their return from Brazil. Sternberg, who was Goethe's contemporary, shared his dedication to the systematic gathering of empirical evidence combined with a search for the unity of nature across the disciplines. Like Goethe and Humboldt, he was also committed to cross-border collaboration to advance scientific knowledge. His treatise *Versuch einer geognostisch-botanischen Darstellung der Flora der Vorwelt*[7] (*Attempt at a Geological-Botanical Representation of Primeval Flora*), the first comprehensive scientific analysis of fossil plants, is still revered today as a path-breaking work in paleobotany.

On 28 April 1820, when he was visiting the spa at Eger in Bohemia, Goethe's diary recorded the stunning news that a fossilised forest of palm trees had been found underground in a nearby district. "The underground palm forest that was discovered in Bohemia came up for discussion. The pit is located in the Pilsen district… and belongs to Count Sternberg." Eager to obtain samples of the fossils, Goethe directed his first inquiry to museum director von Schreibers: "In the Pilsen district, between Cernowitz and Radnitz on an estate belonging to Count Sternberg," his letter of 10 May 1820 explained, "an extraordinary petrified primeval forest has been found that is said to contain palm trees, colossal ferns and perhaps even casuarinas, the details of which are certainly known to you." A few weeks later, he wrote to Kaspar von Sternberg himself to express his interest in obtaining some of his representative fossil samples, adding that his age and state of health made a visit to the site difficult for him. Sternberg was happy to oblige and sent him some plant fossils along with the first published instalments of his *Primeval Flora*. There he argued that the presence of carbonised plant imprints in his coal mine, whose forms were entirely foreign to the endemic plants of the region, seemed to indicate that under different, warmer climatic conditions Northern Europe may have harboured an entirely different type of vegetation. After undertaking an extensive analysis of the petrified vegetation samples found in the coal deposits of his native Bohemia and comparing them to plant fossils found in other parts of Northern Europe, Sternberg concluded that the carbonised tree and plant remains pointed to the transformation of vegetal matter into bituminous coal in an earlier geologic era. To support his conclusions, he referred to the recent identification by Humboldt and the Brazilian travellers of a large number of palm species in the warm, balmy climate of the tropics that appeared to be similar in shape to the subterranean flora found in his Bohemian homeland.

Fascinated as he was by the underlying scheme of plants, or what he called the "Urpflanze," Goethe was thrilled by Sternberg's discoveries and suggested a meeting in the nearby resort town of Marienbad. During the summer of

1822, both men spent the most part of July living under the same roof there. Their daily discussions and their mutual study of Sternberg's fossil collection sealed a scientific friendship that would become, in addition to his friendship with Carl Friedrich Zelter, one of the main solaces of Goethe's old age. The evidence unearthed by Sternberg of fossilised subterranean vegetation seemed to corroborate Goethe's Neptunist belief in a primeval flood and a process of slow sedimentation. Studying the shape and structure of the petrified flora, both noted a morphological analogy to the living, lush vegetation of the tropics. After Sternberg's departure, Goethe shared the exciting news with several of his friends: "Count Kaspar Sternberg," he wrote on 8 August 1822 to Carl Friedrich Zelter, "possesses important coal mines in which the strangest plants are preserved; similar in structure only to the southernmost vegetation, they point to the earliest epochs of the Earth." Not only did Sternberg's fossilised evidence open a window into the Earth's most distant past, the similarity found between the plant fossils and the vegetation of the tropics pointed to past climate change across the Northern Hemisphere. In the following decade, both friends exchanged frequent letters, whose contents moved from the scientific and administrative to the personal. However, the morphological analogy that had sparked Goethe's interest in Sternberg's paleontological research stayed in the forefront of their communication, as highlighted in an agenda notation Goethe made before Sternberg's second visit to Weimar. There again, a full ten years after the first German expeditions to Brazil, we find noted among others in a list of topics for the 11 June 1827 meeting the telling connection between the fossilised underground plants and the live Brazilian vegetation: "Underground Flora. Brazilian Flora."

Carl Friedrich Philipp von Martius

The illustrious Alexander von Humboldt penned a much-quoted aphorism celebrating Carl Friedrich Philipp von Martius's palm tree research: "As long as we name palms and know palms, the name of Martius will be renowned." Humboldt and Bonpland were well placed to appreciate the Bavarian naturalist's achievements, since their own identification of New World trees had expanded significantly the number of known palm species. Returning to Munich after a journey of more than three years from April 1817 to December 1820, which included a 10,000-kilometre-long exploration of Brazil, Martius and Johann Baptist von Spix brought back a huge number of specimens acquired during those years, including 6,500 new plant species and 3,451 dissected animals, as well as a vast ethnographical collection. In recognition of this achievement, King Maximilian I Joseph of Bavaria knighted them and funded the publication of their travel report with a generous stipend. Martius was named a member of the Bavarian Academy of Sciences at the young age of 26. A few years later, he would become Professor of Botany at the University of Landshut. His travel companion, the zoologist Johann Baptist von Spix, unfortunately died in 1826 from the after-effects of a tropical disease contracted during the trip.

After his return from Brazil, Martius launched three simultaneous publishing projects: the famous *Historia Naturalis Palmarum (Natural History of Palms)*, known also as *The Book of Palms*, a richly illustrated monograph on palm species in their natural habitat; *Nova Genera et Species Plantarum quas in itinere per Brasiliam* (*New Genera and Species of Brazilian Plants*), a description of all the botanical specimens collected in Brazil; and a three-volume travelogue, co-authored with Spix, *Reise in Brasilien in den Jahren 1817 bis 1820* (*Travels in Brazil in the Years 1817–1820*).[8] Goethe acquired all these works for his personal library. In later years, Martius also coordinated the publication of the *Flora Brasiliensis* (*Brazilian Flora*), a comprehensive description of Brazilian vegetation. Compiled from 1840 to 1906, and brought to completion long after his death, these 15 volumes constitute the largest botanical project ever undertaken.[9] Taken together, these monumental publishing ventures remain a lasting tribute to his astonishing work output, his organisational genius and his consummate literary skills.

In its self-confident manner, Martius's letter of 23 October 1823 introducing himself to Goethe set the tone for what became a mutually enriching interaction between the younger and the older natural scientists. Claiming some of the credit for the naming of the *Goethea* by Wied-Neuwied and Nees von Esenbeck, Martius praised in glowing terms Goethe's *Metamorphosis of Plants* as the "star illuminating" his and his travel companion's exploration of tropical nature. Two enclosures accompanied his letter which could not have failed to impress its recipient:

an illustrated section of *The Book of Palms* containing lithographs of a variety of palm trees in their Brazilian environment and a handwritten sample of the German introduction to the palm book, titled "Einiges von den Palmen naturgeschichtlich und morphologisch" ("Some Information about Palms, Their Natural History and Morphology"). Adopting Goethe's visual approach to vegetal description with its central morphological formula "all is leaf," Martius discussed the growth of palms as metamorphosed leaves, observing that while the stem of the palm tree grows in a vertical direction, florescence occurs at the top in a spiral pattern of gradation. That double growth model of the palms recognised by the Brazilian explorer was used by Goethe in his 1831 essay on the "spiral tendency" of plants.

Endowing the upward striving of the palm tree with symbolic meaning, Martius called it a "vegetable phoenix," an innocent "bride" in implicit contrast to the luxuriant vegetation and the crawling amphibian and reptilian world of the tropical forest. His introductory essay also postulated that in their natural history palm trees date back to an earlier geological era when, under warmer climatic conditions, they were able to spread to the Northern Hemisphere, a hypothesis that Goethe had seen confirmed by Sternberg's palm tree fossils. Martius's letter also included a request that Goethe review his work, a task the older man immediately began to undertake with the help of his artist collaborator Johann Heinrich Meyer, publishing the piece a year later in his periodical *Hefte zur Morphologie* (*Morphological Notebooks*).

Before visiting Weimar in September 1824, Martius also sent Goethe a copy of the speech he had delivered on the occasion of the 25th anniversary of the Bavarian king's reign. Goethe read it immediately and again just before Martius's arrival. To prepare for the botanist's visit, Goethe also immersed himself in Martius's morphological introduction to the palm book as well as in his own review of the scientist's publications. Martius's speech *Die Physiognomie des Pflanzenreiches in Brasilien*[10] (*The Physiognomy of Flora in Brazil*) is both a precise regional description of the vegetation of Brazil and a masterpiece of stylistic sophistication. It reveals a panoramic display of a pristine landscape with thick virgin forests in the north and prairie and alpine mountaintops in the centre and south of the country, where since the dawn of time plants had ruled unimpeded by human interference. It shows plant growth in the wetlands of the Amazon River basin engaged in a cycle of perpetual unrest and fermentation. The rainforest is described in grim, frightening terms, "dark as hell" and "muddled as chaos," but the southern provinces, with their light forest growth and low-growing plants with rows of palm trees rising above the prairie landscape like classical columns, are coloured in lighter, almost idyllic tones. Pointing to the salt content found in various locations in the inland waters, Martius also suggested that the Brazilian land mass had formerly been submerged by slowly receding seawaters. This empirical observation was congenial to Goethe's Neptunist belief in sedimentary rock formation.

Martius arrived in Weimar before noon on 13 September

1824 and left that same evening. His visit and the topics of the long afternoon conversation are recorded with an unusual wealth of detail in Goethe's diaries:

> Mr. von Martius. Right away a discussion of locales in Brazil, palm trees and other species that yielded splendid insight. He then drove to Belvedere. I prepared for a conversation. He had dinner with us, along with his young wife and her aunt, a Miss von Stengel. I had hung up a large map of Brazil. He went over it all with me. Also the two instalments of the palm treatise that I already owned. In addition he discussed in detail the newest leaves, numbering 100. He told me much about Brazilian conditions. Then the conversation touched on the Botanical Society of Regensburg, and also those of Bonn and Erlangen. I found all his judgements and opinions to be very worthwhile. He stayed until eight o'clock in the evening and I was loath to let him go.

This passage shows both men intensely focused, first on the palm illustrations, then on the study of the Brazilian map, followed by a discussion of Brazilian conditions and of current developments in the scholarly botanical world. Two brief personal sentences stand out: "I had hung up a large map of Brazil. He went over it all with me." They show not only that the vicarious traveller had assiduously prepared himself for the encounter with the Brazilian explorer, but that he studied the map with him, eager to identify and immerse himself in the foreign "localities" visited by Martius. Most likely they would have followed the itinerary of his trip through Brazil: from Rio de Janeiro and São Paulo through the interior of the country and the gold and diamond mining province of Minas Gerais, where the Bavarians had spent time with their compatriot Eschwege, before proceeding northwards toward the Amazon River system for the last legs of the long journey, which extended in a western direction to Peru for Spix and in a northern direction to the Spanish border for Martius.

After Martius left him, Goethe read the first volume of his *Travels in Brazil* and he continued to read it each day during the following week. In 1828 and 1831, he also acquainted himself with the second and third parts of Martius's and Spix's voluminous travel narrative.

Goethe's double commentaries on Martius's *The Book of Palms* – a review included in his *Morphological Notebooks* and a posthumously published essay – highlight the crucial role of pictorial representation that he ascribed to scientific work. In that respect, these brief texts create an interesting parallel to his pictorial transposition of Humboldt's *Essay on the Geography of Plants* in his drawing of the *Comparative Heights of the Old and the New World*. While in that instance Goethe supplemented a missing plate with his own visual design, in the case of his essay on Martius's palm study, he augmented the illustrations and their Latin botanical nomenclature with descriptive German-language captions. In all their brevity, the descriptions of the ten palm lithographs show a similar focus on the interplay of word and image, indicating a recognition of the primacy of pictorial representation for the popularisation of science. By enhancing the visual appeal of the botanical tree samples for the non-specialised reader, Goethe's explanations seek to diminish their geographical distance, making it easier for the reader to identify with them. Through its very immediacy, Goethe concludes, the hybrid medium enables the reader "to feel present and at home in a far-away part of the world," echoing his reaction to Wied-Neuwied's animal illustrations (see Figure 11).

Goethe's review of Martius's palm monograph makes cursory mention of his "already well-known" *Travels in Brazil*, to which he had devoted a great amount of reading time directly following Martius's first visit. The comment is more significant for what it does not say than for what it highlights. Praising the sublime grandeur of the natural scenes of "a great expanse of the world, grandiose, free and open," it skims over the information about "individual occurrences" imparted by Spix and Martius, neglecting to mention their detailed documentation of the flourishing Brazilian economy, which was, of course, enabled by the increased importation of enslaved people from Africa and the growing colonial displacement of the Indian peoples. Since the Bavarian naturalists' travel narrative was composed as both a geographical and ethnological account, the evasiveness of Goethe's language draws attention to its serious omissions. In their portrayal of ethnic diversity in Brazil, and in their discussion of the black slaves and native Indians, the travellers pursued a double-pronged strategy. On the one hand, they realistically showed how the modernisation of the new Brazilian empire in the early 19th century was dependent on the extensive use of enslaved labourers in all economic realms and how the colonial expansion by the Portuguese settlers pushed the indigenous peoples further and further away into the depths of the rainforests. On the other hand, they neutralised their own and their readers' conscientious objections by defending the supremacy of white people over the "degenerate" native and slave populations with a mix of religious, moral and physiological arguments, or elsewhere they concealed the inherent violence of the "Brazilian conditions" under a veil of patriarchal benevolence.

Reports on Martius's second visit to Weimar between 4 and 6 October 1828 indicate that it included a discussion of the sensitive issue of colonial and interracial dynamics. While Goethe's diaries inform us of the scientific and botanical focus of the visit, their talk must have taken a different turn, particularly on 5 October prior to Martius's departure, as shown by Goethe's cryptic commentary: "The conversation was very trenchant, with all the problems of the earliest beginnings of geology and organic physiology being discussed playfully and with an eye to paradoxes." According to a lengthier account of the conversation, recorded by Eckermann after Martius left, the discussion proceeded from the performance of Rossini's *Moses* in the Weimar theatre to the Old Testament, and then to the subject of human origins and the global diversity of races. At this point Martius's monogenist beliefs clashed with Goethe's polygenetic, evolutionist views. To Martius, who defended the biblical account of Adam and Eve as the origin of the human species, which he found compatible with the scientific principle of the natural order, Goethe responded that nature is prodigal and must have created, instead of one single pair of humans, dozens or hundreds of them, wherever natural conditions made it possible. Martius responded that, as a good Christian, he could not agree with a view that contradicted the teachings of the Scriptures. The biblical beliefs expressed by Goethe's guest come to the fore in the *Travels in Brazil*, where the authors' racist portrayal of the native Indians and the enslaved Africans is influenced by the theory of the lost tribes of Israel and the "degeneration" of their descendants.

Goethe's Faust II

At almost the same time as he absorbed Martius's rationalisation of the Brazilian racial hierarchy, Goethe had access to alternative narratives of New World developments. In February 1827, he read the *Political Essay on the Island of Cuba* recently completed by Alexander von Humboldt, with its impassioned indictment of the slave-holding economies of the Caribbean Islands, the southern United States and Brazil. Shortly after that, he assisted in the publication of Duke Bernhard of Sachsen-Weimar-Eisenach's journals from his travels through North America, with their eyewitness portrayal of life on the plantations of the southern United States. The anthropological and social implications of the travel narratives from the New World challenged Goethe for over a decade and were ultimately transposed into the imaginary realm of the second part of his lifelong work on *Faust*, his allegory of the modern transformation of the world. In 1825 he again took up the manuscript of his "classical-romantic phantasmagoria," begun in 1800, and expanded it into the five-act poetic creation *Faust II*, which became the central literary endeavour of his final years.

While the drama's geological features and powerful imagery of nature owe much to the author's armchair voyages into Spanish America, Brazil and the United States, the global reach of Faust's relentless activity in alliance with Mephisto's demonic powers would hardly be conceivable without the author's exposure to the modern transformation of the Americas. The brutal force of the process of European colonialisation is symbolised and intimated within the expansive framework of *Faust II* through two major clues: the extraction of mineral riches powered by the exploitation of slave labour, and the dislocation of the indigenous population from their native lands. The mining of gold hidden in the depths of the mountains – which involved the total instrumentalisation of the weaker by the stronger species – although shielded from representation in the political court scenes of *Faust II*, manifests itself in all its brutal force in the animal world of Greek mythology. In the Philemon and Baucis scenes of the fifth act, Faust's restless and insatiable drive and his alliance with Mephisto's satanic powers add another component to the same dynamics: the forceful removal of native inhabitants from their natural environment. While the play's multiple mythological and allegorical veils conceal the specificity of the locale by lending it an aura of timeless, repetitive generality, the allegorical scenes also bring to the fore the ruthless brutality that energises the process of modern transformation. Informed and nourished by a wealth of contemporary travel readings, Goethe's *Faust II* offers a parable of violent domination fuelled by a European drive to colonial expansion and enrichment.

To North America with Duke Bernhard of Sachsen-Weimar-Eisenach

During the first 60 years of his life, Goethe appears to have had little interest in North America. All that can be confirmed is that he read various accounts of English travellers, among them the journals of Captain Cook describing his voyages across the Pacific Ocean that took him as far as the west coast of North America, including Alaska.

Nonetheless, it would have been difficult for Goethe not to have absorbed information about the United States during his early years. He noted in his autobiography *Poetry and Truth*, for example, that when he was younger, America was "the Eldorado of those who found themselves in straitened circumstances." Looking back, he reported that the American Revolution aroused much interest among the German public: "One wished the Americans good luck, and the names Franklin and Washington began to sparkle and gleam on the political and martial firmaments." But he added, "I myself and my circle of friends did not concern ourselves with gazettes and the news. We were most absorbed in getting to know human nature; in general, we let individuals go their own way."

It was in his later years that America became one of Goethe's favourite armchair destinations. After he became acquainted with Alexander von Humboldt's reports about his extensive scientific expeditions in Latin America, Goethe began to develop an active interest in the new nations to the north, as well. From that time onward he read numerous books describing the fauna, flora and especially the geological and mineralogical conditions of the New World, such as D.B. Warden's *A Statistical, Political, and Historical Account of the United States of North America*,[1] Parker Cleaveland's *An Elementary Treatise on Mineralogy and Geology... in the United States of America*[2] and *Neue Erdbeschreibung von ganz Amerika*,[3] a translation of the extensive section on the Americas contained in Daniel Fenning's monumental two-volume work *A New System of Geography: or, A General Description of the World: Containing a Particular and Circumstantial Account of All the Countries, Kingdoms and States of Europe, Asia, Africa and America...*[4]

Goethe also had a personal source of information on America in several young Bostonians who were studying in Göttingen and who visited Weimar to make his acquaintance. Among them were the classical philologist Edward Everett, the future diplomat and historian George Bancroft and Joseph Cogswell, who was instrumental in arranging Goethe's donation of a selection of his works to Harvard University and who later became Professor of Geology there. Goethe was indebted to Cogswell for his 1819 article from the *Edinburgh Magazine* "On the State of Literature in the United States". In a letter to him on

29 July 1819, Goethe reported reading it "over and over" because it had given him so much excellent information about how that country's literature was "naturally developing its own qualities." In the late 1820s he read American authors such as Washington Irving and especially James Fenimore Cooper. A great admirer of Cooper's works, he requested that all of them be acquired for the Duchess Anna Amalia Library in Weimar.

Most importantly, Goethe gained up-to-date eyewitness knowledge about North America from the journals kept by the 33-year-old Duke Bernhard of Sachsen-Weimar-Eisenach during his almost year-long travels in the eastern and southern half of the United States in 1825 to 1826. The Duke had given a good deal of thought to his itinerary and he described with great specificity what he saw and experienced.

Goethe and Duke Bernhard's Travel Journals

As the second son of Grand Duke Carl August, with whom Goethe had long been closely associated, Duke Carl Bernhard of Sachsen-Weimar-Eisenach (1792–1862) chose to pursue a military career, serving successively in the Saxon and Dutch armies. At 17 years of age he fought with the Saxons, joining French troops to combat the Austrian army at the Battle of Wagram. He was subsequently praised for his valour by Napoleon, who decorated him with the Order of the Legion of Honour. After the Congress of Vienna in 1815, the number of troops in the Saxon army having been cut by half, Bernhard entered the service of the King of Holland. As the commander of a Dutch division, the Duke played a pivotal role in the battles of Quatre-Bras and Waterloo. In 1825–1826, Bernhard was granted leave from his military duties so that he could travel to the United States. He ended his career as commander of the Dutch East Indies army in Java.

In 1811, as a young man, Bernhard had accompanied his father on a journey to Vienna and Graz in Austria and Bologna in Italy, with a follow-up trip in 1812 to Rome to view the city's antiquities. In 1823 he spent several months in England, Ireland and Scotland visiting commercial and military installations as well as a number of natural history museums and art collections.

His next destination was North America which, he later said, he had wanted to visit ever since his youth. During his trip he kept a careful record of his experiences, describing them copiously in a series of journals which he sent back to his parents (see Figure 12).

As Goethe spent a good deal of time enthusiastically following Bernhard's travels, it is pertinent to focus on the Duke's journals here. Indeed, feeling that they would be of interest to a wider circle of readers, Goethe urged the Duke to consider allowing them to be published, proposing that the historian Heinrich Luden be asked to help with the necessary editorial preparation. Luden accepted the task and the journals came out in 1828, in two volumes of more than 300 pages each, as *Reise Sr. Hoheit des Herzogs Bernhard zu Sachsen-Weimar-Eisenach durch Nord-Amerika in den Jahren 1825 und 1826.* An English translation, *Travels through North America, During the Years 1825 and 1826 by*

His Highness, Bernhard, Duke of Saxe-Weimar-Eisenach, followed in the same year.[5]

Beginning with his departure from Ghent for Antwerp on 4 April 1825, the Duke kept a journal every day, covering not only his journey by ship from Belgium to England but also his voyage across the Atlantic, which lasted more than a month; his travels in North America from July 1825 to June 1826; and even the weeks at sea heading homeward. He made sure to send the journals to Weimar at regular intervals. In a brief foreword penned for the published version of the journals, the Duke noted: "I wanted to see the New World, the land and the people, their way of life and institutions, their manners and customs. The more I got to know the Old World, the greater yearning I had to see the new one." His intent had not been to write for a larger audience, but simply for "my esteemed parents, my relations and friends, in order more easily to tell them everything they wished to know."

From Bernhard's journals, it becomes clear that he had read much of the available literature about North America before he arrived on its soil. At various times he mentions Chateaubriand's early chronicles of American scenery and life; Pennsylvanian lawyer and author H.H. Brackenridge's writings about the American Revolution and the frontier; geographer and geologist Henry Schoolcraft's descriptions of Arkansas and Missouri; Friedrich Schmidt's 1822 *Versuch über den politischen Zustand der Vereinigten Staaten*[6] (*Essay on the Political Situation of the United States*); and others. During his trip on the Mississippi and Ohio rivers, he carried with him Samuel Cumings' *The Western Navigator;*

Containing Charts of the Ohio River... and of the Mississippi River, from the Mouth of the Missouri to the Gulf of Mexico...[7] which yielded many details not only about the rivers but also about the surrounding country and towns along the route. On his trip through Ohio, Bernhard often referred to John Kilbourn's *The Ohio Gazetteer: or, Topographical Dictionary, Containing a Description of the Several Counties, Towns [etc.]... in the State of Ohio...*[8] The Duke also frequented bookshops in the cities and towns he visited, often pleasantly surprised by their unexpected existence.

Having been warned before setting off on his journey that Americans would let him know in no uncertain terms that his royal rank meant nothing to them, the Duke arrived in Boston on 26 July 1825 with some trepidation. He reassured himself that he was accustomed to that kind of attitude from his time in the army, particularly in his dealings with the Ministry of War, and he remained determined to see as much of the United States as possible. To his amazement, just two hours after his arrival he found himself the object of "the finest attention of the estimable residents," several of whom offered him "the most excellent hospitality." Bernhard's two-week stay in Boston proved to be representative of how he would conduct and record his entire journey. Curious about everything, he explored the city exhaustively, meeting with dignitaries and officials of all kinds, visiting many different institutions – schools, hospitals, prisons, libraries, museums and the capitol building to mention a few – and viewing Revolutionary War sites such as Bunker Hill, which he described in extensive detail. He became acquainted with residents of all sorts, including his "polite" innkeeper host Colonel Hamilton, who had served in the volunteer military during the Revolutionary War and retained his rank; the mayor of Boston, Josiah Quincy, who guided him around the city and introduced him to his family and friends; and Edward Everett, Goethe's acquaintance from Boston, now Professor of Greek at Harvard College in Cambridge, who gave him a tour of the institution's facilities.

While travelling west from Boston through Massachusetts in the company of a young Dutch ship designer by the name of Tromp, Bernhard stopped in Northampton, where he met two of Goethe's other acquaintances, Joseph Cogswell and George Bancroft. Together they had founded the Round Hill School for Boys there, modelling it on the highly regarded German boarding school Schulpforta in Saxony. In Springfield, the Duke visited the federal armory and the separate manufacturing complex associated with it, which produced 15,000 rifles a year for the American military. After describing the weapons and the manufacturing process, the Duke mused in his journal that it might be less costly to entrust the production work to a private company, as was done in other countries, rather than to have it supported completely by the government.

After a week in Albany, New York, Bernhard continued westward on the almost completed Erie Canal (see Figure 13) to Schenectady, Utica and Rochester, noting that most towns, even small ones, had "two churches, Episcopal/Anglican and Presbyterian, a school, and often a bookstore (for me, a real joy)." Disembarking at Buffalo, where the canal met Lake Erie, he went on to Niagara Falls, about which he had already read a great deal. Impressed by their size and grandeur, he noted many facts about the falls, such as their height and the distance from the American to the Canadian side, describing as well the experience of viewing both sides of the falls from the vantage point of Goat Island, situated between them in the Niagara River where it thundered over the cliffs.

From Lewiston, New York, where the Niagara River flowed into the lake, Bernhard headed eastward, covering 200 miles by steamer on Lake Ontario and continuing up the St. Lawrence River to the cities of Montreal and Quebec. During three days in Montreal he explored the city, finding it rather provincial, but he enjoyed attending a ball there in the home of a well-to-do young couple, even though the women with whom he danced "all spoke the local bad French." In Quebec he visited the Plains of Abraham, describing in his journal the crucial battle between the French forces led by the Marquis de Montcalm and the English troops under General Wolfe, a struggle in which both lost their lives. The French also lost their sovereignty, not only over the city but over the entire colony.

Returning to Montreal, the Duke journeyed south from there to Lake Champlain and, following the lake, back to New York State. He visited the Shaker colony of New Lebanon, founded by Ann Lee, an advocate of the principles of communal property, celibacy and the worship of God by dancing. The town and all its buildings, he noted

Figure 3

Goethe Walking in the Garden behind his House. Lithograph by Daniel Maclise first published in the March 1832 issue of *Fraser's Magazine*, based on a sketch drawn by William Makepeace Thackeray during his stay in Weimar. Perhaps because Thackeray's rendering of Goethe's face was somewhat unflattering, Maclise used the visage from Joseph Karl Stieler's portrait of the German author that had been published in 1828.

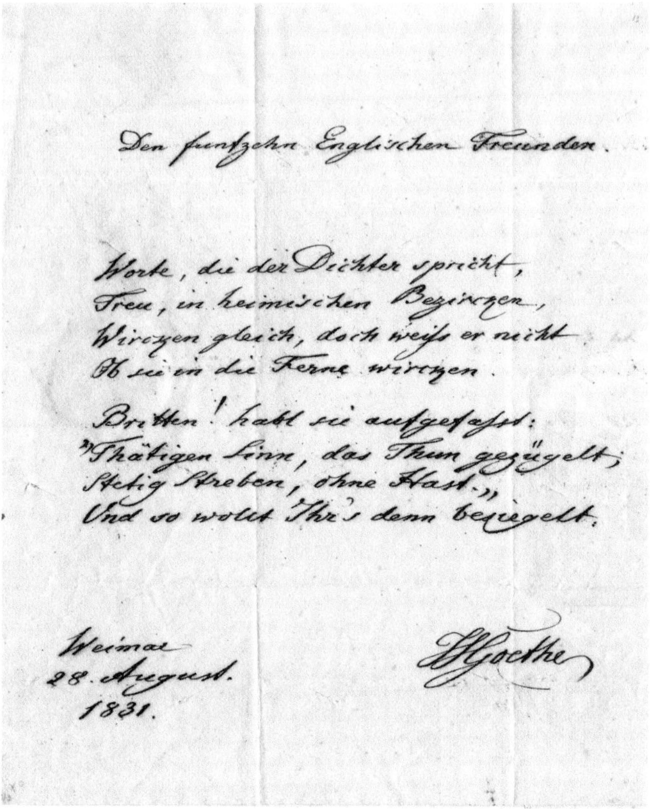

Den funfzehn Englischen Freunden.

Worte, die der Dichter spricht,
Treu, in heimischen Bezirken,
Wirken gleich, doch weiß er nicht
Ob sie in die Ferne wirken.

Britten! habt sie aufgefaßt:
„Thätigen Sinn, das Thun gezügelt;
Stetig Streben, ohne Hast."
Und so wollt Ihr's denn besiegelt.

Weimar
28. August.
1831.

JWGoethe

Figure 4

"Den funfzehn Englischen Freunden," a poem handwritten by Goethe in thanks for a gift sent to him on his 82nd birthday by admirers in England.

Figure 5

The Hafez-Goethe monument by Ernst Thevis and Fabian Rabsch at the Beethoven Square in Weimar.

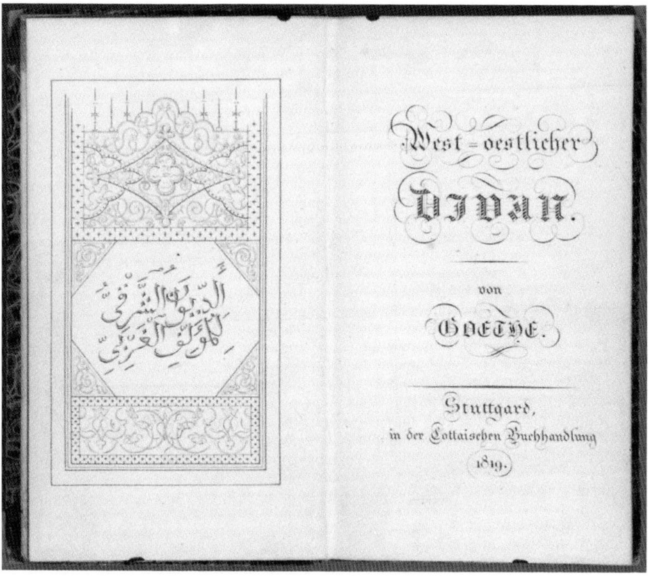

Figure 6

Proof copy of the title copperplate of the original edition of Goethe's *West-Östlicher Divan* with its juxtaposed Arabic and German characters, received by its author on 10 October 1818.

Figure 7

Höhen der alten und neuen Welt bildlich verglichen (*Comparative Heights of the Old and the New World*), pencil drawing by Goethe, with watercolouring by Johann Heinrich Meyer, Weimar 1807, 35.4 × 47 cm.

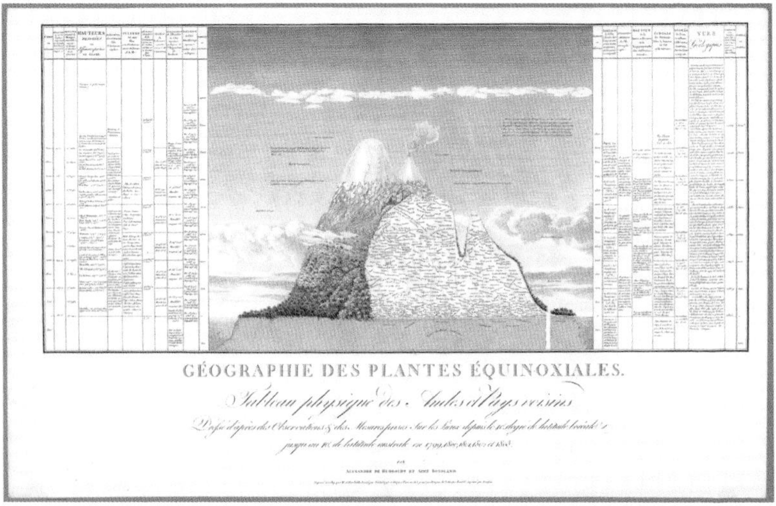

Figure 8

Alexander von Humboldt and Aimé Bonpland, *Géographie des Plantes Équinoxiales. Tableau physique des Andes et Pays voisins* (*Geography of Equatorial Plants: Physical View of the Andes and Neighbouring Countries*), design and composition by Humboldt, drawing by Schönberger and Turpin, engraving by Bouquet, Paris 1805, 37 × 80.5 cm.

Figure 9

The black-and-white print, *Höhen der alten und neuen Welt bildlich verglichen* (*Comparative Heights of the Old and the New World*), of the etching by Johann Christian Starcke was published in May 1813 as the illustrated title page of the 41st volume of the *Ephemerides*, accompanied by Goethe's description of the origin and purpose of the design. In the foreground of the picture, a stone engraved with a dedication to Alexander von Humboldt represents Goethe's appreciation of the recognition paid to him earlier by the explorer.

Figure 10

Maximilian zu Wied-Neuwied's drawing of *Coluber venustissimus*, which appeared in both his *Travels in Brazil* and Bertuch's *Illustrations Concerning the Natural History of Brazil*. The colourful skin pattern arrested Goethe's attention, as evidenced in his Brazilian love poem published in *On Art and Antiquity*.

IRIARTEA ventricosa.

Figure 11

Goethe's review of Carl Friedrich Philipp von Martius' *Historia Naturalis Palmarum* (*Book of Palms*) contains a description of this image, plate 35 in vol. 2 of the book, depicting the palm tree "*Iriartea ventricosa* overlooking a view of a narrow ravine between high forested hills, out of which a river flows to a small waterfall in the foreground."

Figure 12

Portrait of Duke Bernhard with Niagara Falls in the background, by an unknown artist. The Duke made a special point of visiting the falls, having already heard about them in England. Spellbound by the "enormous mass of water thundering down with an overwhelming roar into the terrible depths," he called them an "awesome work of Nature!"

pag. 127.

Ansicht des Erie Canals über den Geneſsee Fluſs in Rochester.

Figure 13

View of the Erie Canal from the Genesee Bridge at Rochester, New York. Copperplate from the 1828 published volume of Duke Bernhard's journals. The Genesee Bridge was an aqueduct built to carry the Erie Canal over the Genesee River in Rochester. Completed in September 1823, it became one of the marvels of the canal. With the advent of the waterway, the city of Rochester flourished, to the point of being dubbed "The Young Lion of the West."

Figure 14

Carl Friedrich Zelter. Drawing after an oil painting by Carl Begas, 1827. The Berlin building contractor and composer Carl Friedrich Zelter became Goethe's closest friend during the last three decades of his life.

Figure 15

Goethe at the age of 68, one year after he decided not to undertake any more lengthy travels. Engraving by Johann Müller after a chalk drawing by the Weimar court painter Ferdinand Jagemann.

Figure 16

The title page of Thomas Carlyle's *Leben Schillers* (*The Life of Friedrich Schiller*) published by Heinrich Wilmans in Frankfurt in 1830, featuring Carlyle's residence in Craigenputtoch, Scotland, based on a watercolour painting by the Scottish author and law professor George Moir.

with some surprise, were immaculate, and he marvelled that this cleanliness extended even to the quarters of the "exceptionally attractive swine," making it "an uncommon pleasure to walk in a Shaker pigsty!"

From New Lebanon he travelled down the Hudson River, stopping for three days at the United States Military School in West Point, which had been founded in 1801 under President Thomas Jefferson. This institution was of particular interest to him as a military officer, and he devoted ten pages in his journal to a precise description of it, even including the daily schedule followed by the cadets "from dawn to dark," along with a lengthy table listing the numerous subjects they were required to take and the books they used.

Continuing down the Hudson to New York City, the Duke found so many other travellers there that he had to make do for his first evening with a "miserable sleeping chamber" in a "dreadful inn." The next day he was able to move to quarters in a "French boarding house" on the outskirts of the city, where he stayed for a week until he eventually found "splendid accommodation" in the City Hotel on Broadway. He spent almost three weeks exploring New York, observing happily that there were not as many pigs running around its streets as there had been in Albany. Surprised by the large number of churches in the city, he attended services at a different one each Sunday he was there, and was bemused to find himself being urged by Quakers to convert to their beliefs and practices. Acquaintances accompanied him on visits to places like the Civil Hospital, the Institute for Juvenile

Offenders, a "Lunatic Asylum" five miles outside the city, the wharves, Fort Columbus on Governor's Island, the American Museum near City Hall (where he admired an "interesting collection of fishes, all very well conserved"), a "high-school" (he used the American term), theatre performances and soirées.

Bernhard's next stay, in Philadelphia, paralleled the ones in Boston and New York. Perhaps because, as he noted, "many Germans and their progeny" lived there, he seemed to feel very much at home in the city, calling it upon his departure his "dear Philadelphia." He was especially interested in the numerous sites in the area that had played a role in the Revolutionary War and the establishment of an independent United States government. Making the acquaintance at a dinner party of fellow guest John Quincy Adams, the country's sixth president, was a highlight of his stay. The Duke reported that while Adams did not speak very much, "what he says is well said." He also expressed feelings of reverence:

> Seldom in my life have I felt such a true and deep respect as in the moment when that estimable man shook my hand, a man whom 11 million people, or at least the best among them, deemed worthy to govern them.

On 18 October 1825, Bernhard visited the town of Bethlehem, 52 miles to the north of Philadelphia. The community had been founded in 1741 by the Herrnhut Brethren of the Moravian Church, who wished to be able to practise their religious beliefs freely there after having been hounded out of Saxony. Bernhard felt he could not leave the state of Pennsylvania without having seen this communal settlement of about 700 persons, mostly artisans and shopkeepers and their families, which had initially been supported by Count Nikolaus von Zinzendorf of Saxony and had become known for its piety and good works. He reported that, although property was not held in common there, the community willingly helped those who were in need. A boarding school provided not only local girls with a good education but also accepted students from around the country. Boys were schooled in the neighbouring town of Nazareth. Bernhard was impressed by the harmony in which the residents of Bethlehem lived, finding one of the reasons for this accord to be that they were united by the bonds of their faith.

On 25 October Bernhard regretfully left Philadelphia and travelled by steamship to Baltimore, a city established in 1752 when it boasted only ten buildings but that now was home to about 75,000 inhabitants. He admired a large white marble monument honouring George Washington, and another dedicated to the citizens of Baltimore who had died defending the city in a battle on 12 September 1814, and noted that there were "many attractive public buildings," among them especially several churches. To view the site where a combination of armed citizens and the military had defeated the British in the 1814 battle, he went to star-shaped Fort McHenry, located two miles south of the city on land jutting out into Chesapeake Bay. He also visited many institutions in the city, including an almshouse, a steam-powered grain mill, a museum and the public library, where he was pleased to be shown a copy of "Humboldt's splendid work on *Mexiko.*" He also found the city's genteel social functions to be "uncommonly pleasant."

Saying farewell to "friendly Baltimore," he journeyed from there to Washington, D.C. on a stagecoach, noting that the dwellings of slaves he passed were "poorer than the least log cabin in New York," and their clothes were very ragged and poor.

Washington fell rather short of the Duke's expectations for a capital city: The Capitol Building itself was "impressive," but it was surrounded by "shabby houses and fields" that did not give evidence at that point in time of the "colossal plan" which had been conceived for the city. Bernhard felt the capital should have been located farther inland, perhaps in West Virginia, to render it safe from marauding enemies, as the British had reached and burned it with ease in the War of 1812. Nonetheless, he liked the people he met in the city, many in the diplomatic corps or in government, and was very pleased to be invited along with 40 other guests to a dinner with President Adams. Together with some new friends, he visited Mount Vernon to pay homage to George Washington. He was particularly interested in the Patent Office, inspecting with fascination the many detailed plans and models of inventions, especially those that made use of new technologies.

Having read Thomas Jefferson's descriptions of the beauties of Virginia, Bernhard travelled from Washington in rickety coaches and often on "very bad roads" to the western part of the state in order to view the Natural Bridge, a famed geological formation in the Blue Ridge mountain area. The difficult trip proved to have been worthwhile, for he declared the span to be "the most magnificent work of nature," more impressive even than Niagara Falls or Mount Vesuvius. Before leaving Virginia, he also visited the University of Virginia in Charlottesville as well as its founder, the former President Jefferson, now 86 years old but "still of sound mind and vision," at Monticello, his residence. From there he continued via Norfolk and Fayetteville to Columbia, the capital of South Carolina, and then on to Charleston, observing the increasing presence of slaves the further south he went.

Bernhard's description of his trip through the South from Charleston to New Orleans indicates that it was the most arduous part of his entire journey, although he enjoyed becoming familiar with the "exceptionally beautiful" native plants and trees, such as "splendid live oaks, laurel trees, magnolias, yuccas and latanier palms." He notes that the further westward he travelled in the South, the more he found the citizens of those states to be less educated than their counterparts in the North. In Milledgeville, at that time the capital of the state of Georgia, the inhabitants seemed to him to be living "cut off from the civilised world."

Familiar as he was with Goethe's views on the usefulness of travel reports as well as with his *Italian Journey*, Bernhard worked at keeping his own reporting style detailed and factual. A keen observer, he gave accurate descriptions of seemingly everybody and everything he encountered, not only the cities and towns he visited but also the landscapes through which he travelled, their weather conditions, fauna, flora and geology. He described his various lodgings and modes of travel, technologies that were new to him and the people whom he met, so that family and friends at home could "travel" with him.

The Duke tried specifically to remain nonjudgmental in his journals, such as when he had first seen slaves in Baltimore:

> I do not have the right to comment on this touchy subject. On my trip I have again had the age-old experience that one can easily form erroneous judgements about things concerning which one knows very little, and which one has not seen and scrutinised oneself.

Nonetheless, the brutal treatment of slaves that he observed as he travelled through the South clearly shook him, as is evident in his description of the physical punishment of slaves he witnessed in New Orleans:

> The maximum number of lashes allowed is 39, as in Mosaic law… The poor wretch is stretched out flat on the earth, face down, with hands and feet fastened to four stakes. In this position he receives the lashes. This horrible form of punishment is especially prevalent on the plantations. In fact, on the plantations a cruel discipline is the rule.

He considered the slave auctions that were held in the city to be "scandalous," and he noted on one occasion in Georgia that some of the Creek Indians who owned slaves treated them better than did the white owners. Similarly, he had to admit that he found the practice of "solitary confinement" (he used the English term), common to most of the prisons he visited, "in which all human company is taken from the prisoners, in which they have no work, no movement and almost no fresh air," to be "much crueller than the death penalty."

After waiting out the winter months of February and March 1826 in New Orleans, where he made the acquaintance of many agreeable people but also observed the frequency of drunkenness and even fist fights at public balls, Bernhard travelled by steamboat up the Mississippi to St. Louis, a 13-day journey of 1,150 miles that would have taken three months by land. Greatly impressed by the boat, the Duke called it "new proof of the huge importance of this splendid invention that is a tribute to human ingenuity."

Established in 1763 and populated by French and Canadian settlers who, Bernhard reported, led a rather wild existence and did nothing to civilise the area, St. Louis had become part of the United States as a result of the Louisiana Purchase in 1803. He noted the changes that had occurred since then:

> Many Americans and foreigners have come here, bringing along their assets and their industry and, with the introduction of the steamboat, easy

> communications opened up with cities on the banks of the Ohio River and also with New Orleans, that vital trading centre for the western states.

He added his opinion that "a glance at the map of the U.S. shows what an important place St. Louis is destined to be."

From St. Louis he continued eastward up the Ohio, then north up the Wabash River to New Harmony, a settlement established in 1814 on the Indiana side of the river by Johann Georg Rapp and his followers. In early 1825, the settlement had been purchased by the British social reformer Robert Owen, who planned to found a utopian community there.

Bernhard's description of New Harmony under Owen was thorough and perceptive. He spent ten days in the town in April 1826 among the varied assemblage of people who had come at Owen's invitation to participate in his project. This group included highly educated men and women from the east who had journeyed down the Ohio River on Owen's "boatload of philosophers," and a bunch of ragtag settlers who had been drawn there mainly for the free food. Neither set of people appeared to be particularly interested in performing all the practical activities necessary to sustain the community. Bernhard was intrigued by Owen's experiment to the extent that he appended his own translation of its 14-page "Constitution, Laws and Ordinances" to his journal, but he also predicted that Owen's community "may not last very long." In fact, a footnote in the Duke's published journals reported that it had dissolved almost exactly a year after his visit there.

His interest piqued by what he had learned in New Harmony about the settlement under Rapp, and preferring to travel much of the way by land rather than on the Ohio River in order to see more of the country, Bernhard routed his trip eastward through Ohio to the area just north of Pittsburgh where Rapp and his followers were building a new town they had named "Economy." Contrary to the apocryphal rumours he had heard about Rapp in New Harmony, Bernhard found him to be an impressive figure, who had led his group for 21 years in building prosperous and harmonious communities in three different locations. The Duke noted that community members "have the greatest reverence for the elder Rapp; they call him 'father' and treat him like one." As Bernhard had heard earlier, Rapp's persuasiveness had convinced his followers that it would be beneficial to abstain from marital relations in order to prevent their community of about 700 from becoming too numerous. However, he learned that neither marriage nor such relations were completely forbidden, and "marriages continue to be entered into, and still some children are born." The Duke made further observations:

> Rapp's intention is almost the same as Mr. Owen's: property owned in common and the cooperation of all members of the community in working together for the general good, in which the well-being of each individual is guaranteed. Mr. Rapp, however,

keeps his community together not just with the hope of achieving these goals but also with the bond of religion, which is completely lacking in Mr. Owen's society. The results speak for Rapp's system.

After a week in Economy spent learning about the community and enjoying the familiar German food and wine he was served, Bernhard left on 23 May 1826 to return to Philadelphia for several days, stopping briefly on the way in Bethlehem to fulfil a promise he had made to visit there once more. By the time he arrived back in New York City his travels had covered 7,135 miles. Noting again how "very big" New York was, he was astonished to find that three new churches had been established since he had been there in the previous year. On 16 June 1826 he left the United States for the month-long sea voyage to Liverpool and, after a short stay in England, for home. Arriving on the continent, Bernhard summed up his reaction:

> At 6 in the morning I stepped onto the quay in Ostend and then onto land. At 4 in the afternoon I continued on via Bruges to Ghent. During this journey I remembered a remark that I had often heard in America, namely that nothing makes such an impression on an American who is visiting Europe for the first time as the old monuments that bear witness to centuries long gone and to the prosperity and good taste of earlier generations. I myself, returning from America where everything is new and no one possesses anything but the energetic present and

aspirations for betterment in the future, found this observation confirmed by my own experiences.

Even before the Duke had returned to Weimar, Goethe had been able to read the first of the journals that Bernhard had sent periodically to his family. Writing to Duke Carl August on 4 January 1826, Goethe thanked the father for sending him one of his son's first communications:

> Duke Bernhard's letter is very welcome and enlightening. His understanding and intelligent descriptions of life in the New World offer much food for thought. May I ask you to send me the journals at your convenience? They would inform me about a number of things that I know of only in general.

Several months later, as Goethe's diary entry of 21 May 1826 indicates, he had begun to occupy himself more frequently with the traveller's accounts of his time in North America:

> Professor Zelter, Berlin. John worked on a fair copy of Helena. Began to read Duke Bernhard's diary from Boston. Spoke with Superintendent of Mines Wahl about some medical issues. Then Privy Councillor Stark came. Discussed needing to decide when to undertake a curative stay at a spa. Councillor von Müller about the most recent agricultural assessment, some matters from Strasbourg and other reports. Noon meal alone. I pondered what I planned to work

on, then made the necessary preparations and drew up a draft. Conversation with Mr. Boisserée.

From early July 1826 onward, Goethe devoted an increasing amount of time to studying Duke Bernhard's journals. Numerous notations in his diaries from then until the end of the year bear witness to the depth of his interest in the journals:

3 July: "Duke Bernhard's journal from September 1825 to mid-October."

4 July: "Duke Bernhard's journal through 15. November."

31 August: "Thought about Duke Bernhard's journals in general. Mr. [...], a travelling Irishman, brought a letter and some mineralogical pieces from Mr. Giesecke..."

9 September: "Duke Bernhard. Talked with him about his trip. Hence a map."

12 September: "By myself, read more in Duke Bernhard's travel journal and thought about it."

17 September: "Continued to read the journal of Duke Bernhard."

19 September: "Finished reading the journals of Duke

> Bernhard and then read Warden's description of the United States."

Goethe was intrigued by the Duke's experiences: how he travelled from one town to another in various kinds of conveyances – from elegant steamboats to rough wagons, by stagecoach and on horseback, sometimes even on foot – and by the people he met and the landscapes, plants and geology he described. The multiplicity of churches that had become established in the United States especially fascinated him, and he was impressed by Bernhard's description of the "Harmony-Society's settlement on the Wabash River, led by the Württemberger Rapp." He found the journals so worthwhile, containing as they did perhaps the most extensive information offered by a European about the contemporary United States in the third decade of the 19th century, that he began to urge the Duke strongly to have them published because they would be of interest and value to many readers. By 16 September 1826 the Duke had apparently assented to the suggestion, for on that date Goethe wrote to a friend and colleague, art historian Sulpiz Boisserée: "The uninterrupted diary is of the greatest worth. I have asked him not to present it in sections, but as a whole."

Goethe started discussing the matter with his associates beginning in late September 1826, as chronicled in his diary entries from that time:

> 22 September: "In the evening Professor Riemer... Possible publication of Duke Bernhard's travel descriptions."

23 September: "Mr. Frommann about type samples."

24 September: "Thought about publication of the travel accounts."

6 October: "In the evening Duke Bernhard. I talked with him about his diary and relevant matters. Professor Riemer. Discussed… Duke Bernhard's travel diaries and their publication."

29 October: "Read Mampel's new travel description. Also a bit from Duke Bernhard's journey."

Goethe felt unable to take on the editorial tasks himself, as he was immersed in completing several of his own works, but he persuaded Jena history professor Heinrich Luden to assume those duties. Luden notes in a "Foreword of the Editor" at the beginning of the publication that he made no major changes to the journals other than omitting at the Duke's request some passages that were repetitive, as well as those that had to do with "family affairs, business and money matters, personal circumstances, [and] military subjects," even though Luden himself thought it was "exactly these things that showed the amiable personality of the Duke in the brightest light."

At the 15 September 1826 meeting of the Amalia Masonic Lodge in Weimar, of which both he and Duke Bernhard were members, Goethe hailed his return with the stanzas "Das Segel steigt, das Segel schwillt!" ("The Sail Ascends, the Sail Swells Out!"), which were later published in the *Morgenblatt für gebildete Stände* (*Morning Gazette for Educated Persons*) with a dedication "To the fortunate and enriched returnee, their brother Serene Highness Carl Bernhard, Duke of Sachsen-Weimar-Eisenach, by the confederation of brothers of the Amalia Lodge in Weimar." Goethe's poem may have functioned in part as an early promotion of the later publication of the Duke's journals, mentioning his observant recounting of his experiences, his gift for achieving an easy rapport with those he encountered and his admiration for the industriousness of many Americans. Goethe's poem ended with the recognition that the traveller continued to recall with pleasure his experiences in the new land:

Das Segel steigt, das Segel schwillt!	The sail ascends, the sail swells out!
Der Jüngling hat's geträumt;	Just as the youth had dreamed;
Nun ist des Mannes Wunsch erfüllt,	The grown man's wish has been fulfilled,
Noch ist ihm nichts versäumt.	There's nothing unattained.
So geht es in die Weite fort	And so his ship heads out to sea
Durch Wellenschaum und –Strauß	Through foaming waves and spray.
Kaum sieht er sich am fremden Ort,	Scarcely arrived on foreign shores,
Und gleich ist er zu Haus.	He feels himself at home.

Da summt es wie ein Bienenschwarm,
Man baut, man trägt herein,
Des Morgens war es leer und arm
Um Abends reich zu sein.

Geregelt wird der Flüsse Lauf
Durch kaum bewohntes Land,
Der Felsen steigt zur Wohnung auf,
Als Garten blüht's im Sand.

Der Reisefürst begrüßt sodann,
Entschlossen und gelind,
Als Bruder jeden Ehrenmann,
Als Vater jedes Kind,
Empfindet wie so schön es sei
Im frischen Gottesreich;
Er fühlt sich mit dem Wackern frei
Und sich dem Besten gleich.

It's buzzing like a swarm of bees
With building, hauling loads,
What morning was deserted, poor,
By evening has turned grand.

The rivers' courses are improved
Through barely lived-in land,
The rock becomes a dwelling place,
And gardens bloom in sand.

The travelling prince greets everyone,
Is resolute and mild,
All upright men he treats as friend,
A father to each child.
He feels how wonderful it is
To be in God's new realm;
With all brave men he now feels free
And equal to the best.

Scharfsichtig Land und Städte so	Keen-eyed, observing
Weiß er sich zu beschaun;	Land and town;
Gesellig auch, im Tanze froh,	Convivial, enjoying a dance,
Willkommen schönen Fraun;	And welcomed by the ladies fair.
Den Kriegern ist er zugewöhnt,	At ease with warriors, as well,
Mit Schlacht und Sieg vertraut;	Familiar with the fight and winning,
Und ernst und ehrenvoll ertönt	And with the grave solemnity
Kanonendonner laut.	Of sombre cannon thunder.
Er fühlt des edlen Landes Glück,	He feels the fortune of this land,
Ihm eignet er sich an,	Assumes it as his own,
Und hat bis heute manchen Blick	And even now he still looks back
Hinüberwärts getan.	To where he just has been.
Dem aber sei nun wie's auch sei,	But this is how things are right now,
Er wohnt in unserm Schoß. –	He's back in our embrace. –
Die Erde wird durch Liebe frei,	The Earth becomes, with love, more free,
Durch Thaten wird sie groß.	By deeds it grows in grace.

Goethe sent a copy of the poem to at least one of his correspondents, Count Kaspar Maria von Sternberg, along with added praise of Duke Bernhard's journals. The packet also included items such as "Art and Antiquity Vol 3, dedicated to the benevolent recipient," a "question about an unusual fossil" and "some botanical notes." Goethe added a letter dated 23 September 1826, explaining:

> The enclosed poem greeted our Duke Bernhard upon his safe return from America; the journals he kept continuously during his… trip in the United States are very enjoyable. The newest travel accounts always have the appeal of newspapers; while the latter report on recent events in the world, the former describe contemporary conditions, and because they also have to touch on the past, one can at the same time view constancy, progression and regression.

Goethe continues with regard to Bernhard's journals:

> What I especially admired was the strategy in which the trip was undertaken and executed; nothing was done accidentally or uselessly. The traveller always maintained his equilibrium… and whoever did not know him would have had difficulty guessing who he was. One observes a man of the world… who is welcome everywhere, a well-schooled and tested military man, a participant in state and civil affairs, someone who is at home at every banquet and ball and not insensitive to feminine charms. We are

able to observe his elegance on public occasions, his entertaining conversations, his free-minded decency, conscious of his dignity and using the advantages of his high position to participate in a way of life that is easier and quicker.

Goethe closes his description by observing that, nonetheless, the Duke "does not avoid any inconvenience, indeed he is able, especially when he is travelling, to learn from the often arduous but also companionable circumstances." At less length, but using similar words, on 22 October 1826 Goethe also wrote about the Duke's journals to both his friend Carl Friedrich Zelter and to Wilhelm von Humboldt, brother of the explorer.

Images of the United States in the Age of Goethe

The country of teeming enterprise and restless activity celebrated in the poem "The Sail Ascends, the Sail Swells Out!" dedicated to the Duke, differed from the images of America held in Germany and other European countries during the late 18th and early 19th centuries.

The most prevalent image of America, common to Europeans since Columbus, was that of a "golden land" where no one suffered from a lack of material well-being. Numerous reports about the new continent's wealth of natural resources as well as its remarkable beauty had strengthened this concept over time. A growing knowledge about conditions abroad led gradually to more realistic appraisals, but books and pamphlets written for potential emigrants in the early 19th century revived the dream of an earthly paradise. These emigration primers promised what many people were eager to hear, and thousands began preparing for the long journey across the Atlantic.

America was not just the focus of material longings. The newness and rawness of the country generated an image of America as a land without culture, tending to induce in many Europeans an attitude of superiority or disdain. By the time the Americans had achieved their independence, such patronising assessments had lost much of their credence among Europeans, but in Britain, where resentment over the colonists' defection remained fresh in many minds, negative attitudes continued to prevail well into the 19th century.

Another complex view of America is closely associated with the phenomenon of European Romanticism, particularly after the advent of Jean-Jacques Rousseau. Although America had not influenced Rousseau when he first idealised the state of nature, it served to confirm with him and with the rapidly growing number of his followers their primitivistic concepts. What better prototype for the "bon sauvage" could there be than the Native American, born of the virgin forests of Ohio and Mississippi, untouched by European civilisation? This idealised child of nature came to life in fictional representations of the time, many of which contrasted the disorder of Europe with the harmony of existence to be found in the wilderness abroad.

The existence of America encouraged others to give voice to their political aspirations. Perhaps the most influential of these views held that the United States, after the Revolutionary War, was a prototypical democratic society. This image initially received strong affirmation when Enlightenment philosophers discovered a perfect location in the New World for their vision of building a province of tolerance and liberty. The colonists' declaration of independence and their struggle against the British Crown lent new dimensions to these ideals. Particularly to the middle and lower classes, America – now the United States – appeared to promise political and religious privileges they could never attain in their home countries.

It is likely that Goethe must at least have been aware of, if not sympathetic to, the concept of America as a country without the cultural achievements of Europe. Indeed, much of the information he received until the 1820s about current conditions in America came by way of critical sources. *The Foreign Quarterly Review* and *Blackwood's*, bastions of Tory condescension that played on the theme of Old World superiority, were part of his regular reading. And the French journal *Le Globe*, his favourite source of news from abroad since its first issue was published in 1824, was also initially not always kindly disposed toward America. In addition, Goethe was privy to the confidential letters dispatched by Johann Christian Hüttner, Duke Carl August's agent in London. From 1814 to 1829, Hüttner reported almost weekly on news from England and included numerous items about the United States in his accounts. Hüttner's prejudice condemned everything that originated on the other side of the Atlantic, depicting the Americans as "hypocritical, boastful, given to exaggeration, filthy and ill-mannered in every respect, far below the English standard."[9]

Similarly, two books with which Goethe was familiar drew a dim picture of daily life in America. They were Moritz von Fürstenwärther's *Der Deutsche in Nord-Amerika*[10] (*The German in North America*) and Ludwig Gall's two-volume treatise *Meine Auswanderung nach den Vereinigten-Staaten in Nord-Amerika im Frühjahr 1819 und meine Rückkehr nach der Heimat im Winter 1820*[11] (*My Emigration to the United States in Spring 1819 and My Return Home in Winter 1820*).

Gall's account of his journey, from his passage on a noisome emigrant ship and his subsequent search for a place to make a home to his decision to return to Europe, consisted of a chain of depressing experiences. Upon his arrival in New York he encountered "swindling, unpleasantness and self-interest above everything."[12] In the New Jersey city of New Brunswick, he complained about "a lack of civic virtue, the wellspring of the degeneracy in the United States."[13] Fürstenwärther's book, written in response to the philanthropist Hans von Gagern's demand for an investigation into the fate of German settlers in America, was even more distressing. The author asserted that most immigrants became victims of profiteering agents and brokers, and he came to the conclusion that, in general, Germans in America found their industry, their knowledge, their savings, whatever they had, exploited by others. Many of them lived, "miserable and helpless," feeling like "German slaves on the Ohio."[14]

There is no proof that Goethe accepted these reports

at their face value. But at least he seems to have been impressed by the authors' accounts. This is apparent in his review of Gall's book for the periodical *Über Kunst und Altertum* (*On Art and Antiquity*), in which he compared the writer's tribulations to the experiences of the 16th-century knight errant Hans von Schweinichen and suggested that Gall's account provided much fodder upon which younger German authors could draw for fictional pieces. Of Fürstenwärther's book, Goethe opined in a 9 January 1826 letter to his colleague Chancellor von Müller: "Yesterday evening I ventured a quick glance over this ocean and left forthwith. In general, the work is admirable; it will be better to keep silent… and learn from it." One can deduce from such sources that Goethe knew of the negative reactions to America that were prevalent in his time; although he may not have shared them, there is no indication that more idealised views had much of an impact on him, either.

While Goethe appears to show no particular interest in the constitutional system of the United States as a whole, one aspect of public life in America introduced by the American constitution did seem clearly to have impressed him: he was surprised that no alliance between church and state – the cause, he felt, of so many deplorable events in the European past – had been allowed to develop there. That 90 different Christian denominations existed side-by-side in New York City alone astounded him, and he frequently made mention of this circumstance, which he believed was unimaginable in any other country.

*

Influenced by what he had learned from his armchair travels in Latin America, he also suggested, in a conversation with Johann Peter Eckermann on 21 February 1827, that if one could enhance existing waterways to construct a passage from the Atlantic to the Pacific Ocean to be used by "ships of all sizes carrying every kind of cargo," there would be "incalculable results for civilised and uncivilised peoples." He would be surprised, he said, if the United States "would not seize the opportunity to take on such a task. It is likely that this young country, with its decided tendency to push westward, will in 30 to 40 years have taken possession of the large expanse of land on the other side of the mountains and settled it." He made a prediction based on the presence of "so many large and safe natural harbours along the Pacific coast of the country":

> Gradually very important commercial centres will emerge to advance trade with China and the East Indies. If that should happen, it will not be merely desirable but almost necessary that both merchant vessels and warships have access to a quicker passage between the North American west and east coasts than has been possible so far by making the boring, disagreeable and expensive trip around Cape Horn.

Not focusing solely on America, he added rather pensively:

> I would like to experience this, but I won't… I would

> [also] like to experience a link between the Danube and the Rhine. But this is an undertaking similarly so gigantic, that I don't think it can be carried out, especially considering our German resources. And finally… I would like to see the English in possession of a canal at Suez.

Goethe's Wilhelm Meister

Any influence Goethe's ideas about America might have had on his writings is considered to be found most clearly in his lifelong undertaking, the *Wilhelm Meister* novel. In the best-known, classical version of the novel written and published in the 1790s, *Wilhelm Meisters Lehrjahre* (*Wilhelm Meister's Apprenticeship*), the attraction that an idealised America held for adventurous, young Europeans is invoked, as when Lothario, who goes to serve with the French "under the flags of the United States," sees his hopes of immediate self-realisation disappointed, and returns to his homeland, to his own house and orchard. There, surrounded by family and friends, he exclaims: "Here or nowhere is America!" The idea of opportunities available abroad acts as an inspiration for other characters in the novel too, such as the members of the "Tower Society" who devise a plan to colonise territories in an unspecified land overseas and invite Wilhelm to participate in the project, "for to make a long trip is most useful for a young man."

While the shorter sequel to the novel, *Wilhelm Meisters Wanderjahre* (*Wilhelm Meister's Journeyman Years*), abandoned the idea of emigrating to lands across the seas when it was first published in 1821, a revised and expanded second version completed in January 1829, well after Duke Bernhard's return from North America, again takes up the idea of emigration, with the project assuming new contours. No longer is the idea of relocating an individual pursuit, motivated by activist drive or dreams, but rather a group undertaking spurred by economic necessity, for – as Lenardo, the leader of the group, proclaims – moving on and migrating must become "a habit and a need" for those displaced by automation. A community of weavers threatened by technology finds that mobility is necessary for their economic survival. Thus they cannot help but relocate to find new work opportunities, either within Europe or across the ocean. The availability of land in the vast tracts of untouched wilderness and the freedom of religion to be found overseas are incentives, but the focus in the revised novel shifts from the goal of emigrating to the human qualities required of those who undertake to do so. The emigrants in the *Journeyman Years* must be practical men and women, equipped with specific work skills and an active mindset and dedicated to the goal of serving the needs of their community.

While the new concept of emigration as a group undertaking requiring a strong work ethic and practical skills may show the impact on Goethe's novel of Duke Bernhard's descriptions of the communal settlements he visited in North America, it is doubtful that Lenardo's settlement idea can be attributed to just one single identifiable community. In formulating his concept of what the characteristics of the new communal structure far from the Old World would be, Goethe seems to have used an amalgam of the positive qualities of the communitarian societies described by Duke Bernhard. Simultaneously, Lenardo's categorical exclusion of Jews from the "League of Emigrants," in spite of the future community's commitment to religious tolerance, forces the readers of *Wilhelm Meister's Journeyman Years* to come to terms with the troubling issue of the novel's anti-Judaic aspects.

"America, you have it better"

Although Bernhard's descriptions may have been useful to Goethe as material for his approach to revising the *Journeyman Years*, he was still less focused on social and political conditions in America in general than on obtaining information concerning the natural resources and the geology of the United States, about which Bernhard's journals similarly provided much material. During the last 15 years of his life, Goethe acquired a great deal of scientific knowledge about America, mainly by reading whatever relevant materials became available to him. Again, the catalogue of his library is revealing: it lists only five publications on American life and history, yet there is no lack of books relating to scientific matters – nearly 50 such titles, including nine on botany, 17 on geography, nine on geology and seven on mineralogy and mining, belonged to his collection. That Goethe read almost all of these volumes is documented in the catalogue. Moreover, a similar number of books on scientific aspects of America were checked out in Goethe's name from the ducal library. From this reading knowledge, as well as from correspondence with Cogswell and several other American scientists, Goethe felt justified in deducing – incorrectly – that in the United States there was no basalt, a product of volcanic action. This bolstered his Neptunist concept of the slow evolutionary development of natural phenomena.

Three explicit comments Goethe made about the supposed lack of basalt formations in America are contained in manuscripts that were found among his papers. In the autumn of 1819 he noted: "North Americans lucky to have no basalt." Four years later, after studying Heinrich von Struve's *Beiträge zur Mineralogie und Geologie des nördlichen Amerika's. Nach Amerikanischen Zeitschriften bearbeitet*[15] (*Contributions to the Mineralogy and Geology of North America. Derived from American Magazines*), he touched on the same theme: "That part of the world can be considered lucky in its lack of volcanic influences; it gives the New World a much more solid quality than one finds in the old one, where nothing seems to stand on firm ground anymore."

The third reference is contained in an unposted letter to Carl Friedrich Zelter, which Goethe dictated in June 1827 and which concludes in a spirit of resignation:

> All this should not bother a writer who was already famous in his sixtieth year; but never before have there seemed to be so few readers and so many watchdogs and scrutinisers… Several days ago I indulged in the following lines:

Amerika, du hast es besser	America, you have it better
Als unser Continent das alte,	Than does our continent, the old one.
Hast keine verfallene Schlösser	You have no decaying castles
Und keine Basalte.	And no basalt.
Dich stört nicht im Innern,	You are not disturbed internally
Zu lebendiger Zeit,	At the present time
Unnützes Erinnern	By useless memories
Und vergeblicher Streit.	And futile argument.
Benutzt die Gegenwart mit Glück!	Be happy in the present!
Und wenn nun Eure Kinder dichten	And if your children should turn to writing
Bewahre sie ein gut Geschick	May a good fortune protect them from
Vor Ritter-, Räuber- und Gespenstergeschichten.	Penning tales of knights, brigands, and ghosts.

The poem as a whole does not, as some have asserted, express Goethe's unreserved admiration for the United States. Just as do the other instances in which, over a period of nine years and with almost the same words, he had expressed his envy for the New World as a continent without basalt formations, the poem mainly reflects his annoyance with the Vulcanists rather than an enthusiastic view of all aspects of the New World. And just as political undertones can be detected in his remark that in the Old World nothing seems to stand on firm ground any more, his reference to "decaying castles" might be an indication of his dismay about the revolutionary disturbances in the Europe of his time.

Although the poem later appeared in print under the title "Den Vereinigten Staaten" ("To the United States"), this designation most likely did not stem from Goethe, who included it without a title in his letter to Zelter. It may have been added by a trusted adviser, Friedrich Wilhelm Riemer, who had selected that poem along with six others for publication in the *Musenalmanach für das Jahr 1831* (*Muses' Almanac for the Year 1831*). If he did propose the title, it would not have been the first time in which Riemer zealously made decisions that modified Goethe's intentions.

Even if the evidence of enthusiasm for America seems rather tenuous from his writings, Goethe clearly had an interest in several aspects of the country. This curiosity was nurtured by his reading later in his life and especially by the information he gained from Duke Bernhard's journals. And it could be that by publishing these journals, as Goethe had urged, and by presenting a factual picture of the contemporary United States, Duke Bernhard of Sachsen-Weimar-Eisenach was able, as he had hoped, to contribute to making his contemporaries, including Goethe, more knowledgeable about North America and also to change European and British opinions about it.

Carl Friedrich Zelter Travels for Goethe

Carl Friedrich Zelter was born in Berlin on 11 December 1758 and died there on 15 May 1832, not quite two months after the death of his close friend Goethe. Almost ten years younger than Goethe, he came from a family of craftsmen. Following in his father's footsteps, he became a builder and bricklayer, but he was also strongly drawn to music at a very early age. He taught himself to play various instruments and also began to compose songs. At the relatively late age of 26, he undertook formal instruction in composition, which he studied with the court harpsichordist, Carl Friedrich Christian Fasch. When Fasch – who was also the director of the Sing-Akademie zu Berlin (Berlin Choral Academy), thought to be the world's oldest mixed choir – died in 1800, Zelter was appointed to be his successor. Within a few years, he had transformed the Choral Academy from a group of enthusiastic amateur singers into a serious musical institution. He later commissioned a friend, the renowned architect Karl Friedrich Schinkel, to draw up plans for a building in which the Academy, as well as its affiliated orchestra school, could be housed, not far from the broad avenue Unter den Linden. In 1952, the East German authorities used the building to house the

Maxim Gorki Theatre. The Choral Academy still exists today but at a different location in the eastern part of Berlin.

Zelter was a part of the Second Berlin Lieder School, whose representatives were known less for their own ideas than for their dedication to the poetic expression of the texts they set to music. Zelter generally based the songs he composed on poems by Friedrich von Matthisson, Friedrich Schiller and especially Goethe, who in turn preferred Zelter to all other composers (see Figure 14).

The correspondence between the two started with an initiative on the part of Zelter, who in August 1799 sent one of his compositions to Goethe. He received a friendly, yet noncommittal reply. This exchange would most probably have lapsed, had it not been for a meeting between Zelter and Goethe in Weimar in the spring of 1802. That the two of them clearly enjoyed each other's company is confirmed by subsequent letters in which they discussed personal as well as musical matters. In the years after Schiller's death in May 1805, Goethe turned more frequently to Zelter, and a relationship developed between them based on a deep affection. A formal confirmation of their friendship occurred on 3 December 1812, when Goethe received from Zelter a letter recounting with profound anguish that his adult stepson had died by suicide. In an immediate letter, by return, Goethe addressed Zelter with the familiar "Du," instead of the more formal "Sie" (in the English of today, both words are translated as "you"):

> Your letter, my dear friend, informing me of the great misfortune that has befallen your family, weighed heavily upon me, indeed it left me grief-stricken, for it found me amidst very serious contemplations about life; I was only able to take fresh courage from your example [of trying to rally yourself].

After that, missives travelled regularly between Weimar and Berlin, generally every two to three weeks over the next two decades. The correspondence included news, questions, ideas, observations, thoughts and feelings, as well as a fair amount of gossip. The letters reveal that, in spite of their affinity for each other, Goethe and Zelter had very different personalities: Goethe was a man of contemplation, a writer and researcher who had increasingly created a rather removed existence for himself. Zelter was a bundle of energy, a man of action, who said of himself that he was never more alert and productive than when everything around him was "humming and buzzing."

From his location in the small and relatively quiet city of Weimar, Goethe enjoyed hearing about what Zelter was doing and experiencing in Berlin. He especially liked to get news about performances in the theatres there, and in particular about how they were being staged. Zelter, a lover of both opera and theatre, was happy to oblige. As he knew that Goethe read the newspapers from Berlin, he did not repeat what could be found in their reviews, but added other titbits of interest, which numbered in the hundreds over the years of their correspondence.

Relating to a performance of Grillparzer's *Das Goldene*

Vlies (*The Golden Fleece*), he reported: "Medea agonises, Jason agonises, Creon, Creusa, the midwife all agonise and they all berate each other like fishwives." Of Auber's *La muette de Portici* (*The Mute Girl of Portici*), he declared:

> The girl is mute as a fish, but the others make such a horrible racket, for five long acts, that finally even Vesuvius is awakened and spews forth its innards booming toward the clouds. Our public has already swallowed this titanic repast 27 times – and doesn't tire of it.

Goethe relished Zelter's descriptions and urged him to keep on sending his observations, at times exhorting him not to be too "mild" in his judgements.

Zelter also wrote about Berlin life in general, describing what was happening in the worlds of artisans and small shopkeepers, musicians and artists, as well as at the newly established university (now the renowned Humboldt University named after the Humboldt brothers), and he even included news from the court. Goethe appreciated everything he learned from Zelter about Berlin, once remarking that it was as if the residents of a big city were "invited to an uninterrupted feast," where "one only needs to nibble to become satiated."

Not only did Zelter send Goethe news of the social and artistic feast that was Berlin, but at the latter's request he also sent him culinary items that were not available in Weimar. Cod and shellfish packed in ice made their way to the smaller city, as did turnips (called "Teltower

Rübchen" by the locals) that were apparently not available from anywhere except Teltow, a small town south of Berlin.

Zelter also talked about darker aspects of life in his home city, such as the suffering of the citizens during the Napoleonic occupation or the cholera epidemic of 1831, when he wrote to Goethe:

> Yesterday I was invited to an amiable supper. Fifteen honourable men. Before sitting down at table, we agreed not to talk about the cholera. We stayed there for two hours, and nobody could talk about anything except what we had forbidden.

In sum, Zelter wrote about everything and everybody. Nothing was too exalted for him and nothing too lowly, and nothing that Goethe might like to hear about seemed to escape him.

During the many years in which Goethe and Zelter corresponded, some of Zelter's letters described his travels outside Berlin. The enthusiasm with which Goethe received these reports makes clear how much he liked to participate vicariously in the journeys of his friend, even to the point of involving himself in them as if they were his own (see Figure 15).

Between 1816 and 1827, Zelter undertook eight different journeys, six of which lasted longer than a month. From 16 July to 12 September 1816 he visited southwestern Germany, stopping in Wiesbaden, Heidelberg and Baden. A journey in the summer of 1819 brought him on 7 July to Carlsbad, from where he continued to Vienna via Regensburg and along the Danube River. Having arrived in the Austrian capital, he wished to become acquainted with the city's musical and theatrical offerings, returning home only on 1 October. In 1820, from 18 August until 16 September, he was in Greifswald and Stralsund on the Baltic Sea, as well as on the island of Rügen, continuing from there by boat during a severe storm to Swinemünde (today Świnoujście), then via Stettin (today Szczecin) and Schwedt back to Berlin. The following year Zelter travelled only briefly, from 20 to 25 August, to Kunersdorf (today Kunowice on the German-Polish border). In 1822, for four weeks from 26 May to 26 June, he was in Herrnhut in eastern Saxony near the border with Poland, and then in Bautzen, Dresden and Dessau. His longest journey took place in 1823: he left Berlin on 4 October for Holland to learn more about the country's famed organ-building techniques. He travelled westwards, making various stops to see the sights along his way to Utrecht, Amsterdam and Haarlem; a more southerly return route brought him, among other places, to Weimar, before he arrived back in Berlin on 19 December. He travelled again briefly in 1824, from 9 to 17 October, to Garden near Stettin for the wedding of his son Georg, cheerfully describing the post-ceremony revels in a hot and smoke-filled inn, to which all the guests were confined owing to heavy rain. Zelter's last extended trip was to Munich from 5 September to 16 October 1827. Open to experiences beyond theatre and musical performances, he attended a meeting of natural scientists there at Goethe's behest and reported back to his friend.

During all his travels Zelter wrote to Goethe, usually in a sequence of letters ranging from 7 to 37 pages. Some passages from his 20 July 1819 account of travelling by boat on the Danube River from Regensburg to Vienna are typical of his style. He began with a description of the ship:

> The design of such an ordinary ship is so laughably simple that, instead of feeling it might be dangerous, one climbs on board in order to see what the joke looks like. It is built out of pine using just an axe and a saw, rather like a mock-up of a ship; there is no iron, rigging, hemp, tar, pitch, anchor or anything else used to make a ship navigable.

Zelter also described the other passengers:

> My travelling companions included a medical doctor from Ireland, a German copperplate engraver who delivered very eccentric pronouncements about art and sported a beard around his mouth and chin in the style of the Middle Ages, a pharmacist, a butcher, an armourer, a Capuchin monk, women, children, whores, journeymen and yours truly.

He talked about things that happened during the trip:

> The day labourers, who pay little or nothing for their passage, had agreed to take the oars for two hours each at a time, but their performance of this duty was

> decidedly lacklustre. In the mornings and evenings, when it was cooler, I joined them at the activity, which got things moving, and finally even the women and girls helped with the hard work.

By the trip's end, Zelter was thoroughly enjoying himself:

> Our motley company was soon so cheerful and lively that the six days flew by as if they were six hours. The boatmen had laid on the best Bavarian beer, and we were able to buy meat and bread and wine every morning. To sum up, we could have travelled in this manner all the way to Peterwardein[1] without wishing for anything more.

Testifying to his keen facility for observation, impressions similar to those from his Danube trip can be found in almost all of Zelter's accounts of his travels. They were spontaneous and down to earth, reflecting his irreverent personality.

Parts of Zelter's letters are reminiscent of Goethe's own travel accounts. Like Goethe, Zelter described the people whom he met in succinct sketches; what he says about the passengers on the Danube boat sounds like a variant of Goethe's description of a celebration of Saint Roch in the town of Bingen on the River Rhine. Also like Goethe, Zelter described places that he visited, imparting his initial impressions whether positive or negative. His account of his arrival on 11 October 1827 in Coburg as he was returning from Munich: "The first glimpse of this city indicates that it is prosperous, even though beyond the main streets and squares there are many poorly maintained buildings typical of a mining town…" This description is suggestive of a passage in Goethe's diary at the beginning of his journey to Italy:

> Crossing into Bavaria one comes upon Waldsassen Abbey, situated in a lovely meadow and surrounded by fertile rolling hills. The soil is decomposed argillaceous slate, made friable by the quartz that was contained in the slate but did not break down. The land climbs until Tirschenreuth, and the streams flow toward the traveller in the direction of the Eger and Elbe rivers; beyond Tirschenreuth the land slopes southward, and the streams run toward the Danube.

Zelter's writings about art exhibitions in Amsterdam and Munich echoed Goethe's style in *On Art and Antiquity*. In Amsterdam on 24 October 1823, he noted:

> The public art museum has a wealth of good paintings, most of which are related to this country. In addition to the names Backhuisen, Beerestraten, Berghem, Ferd. Bol, Gerard Dou, VanDyk, Eyk, Flink, Helst, Hondhorst, Kalf, Potter, Pynacker and Rembrand, one also finds a Holbein, a Correggio and an excellent landscape by Ph. Hakkert, in which the figures of people were painted by Adr.v.d.Velde. Outstanding Ruisdals, vander Werfs and Wouwermanns [the spelling of the artists' names

> is Zelter's]. They total not much more than 500 – but all of them are so well preserved, framed and cared for that they should still be there to be enjoyed for centuries.

And in Munich on 18 September 1827:

> The Leuchtenberg Art Gallery houses about 300 paintings by Italian, Spanish, German and French artists both old and new that are definitely worth seeing. In the public rooms, among other works in marble, are the Three Graces and a Magdalene by Canova, parts of which are particularly well done… Unfortunately, in the lower areas of the marble there are blue veins that, even though they are toward the back, disfigure parts that would otherwise be lovely. The armchair from the Tuileries on which Napoleon sat in the Senate is on display here; noticeably, on both sides large and small cuts have been scratched into the arms, all of them betraying signs of impatience. It seems in the greater arena it may be the same as everywhere, just as when in our little Senate I have to listen to things I would not read if they appeared in print. If I am doing an injustice to these hieroglyphics, I still know what I think and you know it, too.

Recognising that Goethe would appreciate it, Zelter included descriptions of nature in his narratives. In the Baden Valley near Vienna, he recorded the various kinds of rock he had found there. On his return trip from Holland, he remarked on an unusual cloud formation that he had seen between Bonn and Neuwied on 14 September 1823:

> An enormous nebulous mass coalesced into a frightening configuration, obscuring the entire solar disk and giving rise to a struggle worth watching. The rest of the sky, clear and bright, was beleaguered by the threatening formation, in battle position, a conflict that continued for quite a while. The drama took place right in front of me, high over the ruins of Hammerstein Castle, in the direction I was riding.

Just as Zelter wished to inform his friend about his experiences, Goethe was eager to thank him for his descriptive letters. He did so with considerable warmth, as when he declared in a letter of 28 August 1816, "I am happy you are having such marvellous experiences and entertainments; you deserve to see the world and enjoy it, because you understand and value it." To demonstrate his gratitude, and because he knew that Zelter did not keep duplicates of his letters or even any notes, Goethe had his secretary copy the letters from some of his friend's trips: on 23 March 1820, for example, he wrote to Zelter to tell him that "I took so much pleasure in the mementos of your summer trip that I thought you might enjoy having them again, too."

On several occasions Goethe told Zelter that in his thoughts he accompanied his friend on his journeys, writing, for example, on 7 October 1819: "How can I thank you enough, my excellent friend, that you allow me to travel with you as a welcome companion, continuously conversing with me."

Goethe was so interested in Zelter's travels that on 30 October 1824 he encouraged his friend to undertake more trips: "I have been hoping for quite a while that you could be urged to journey somewhere else, because I was certain that then I would again hear about your expedition." At times he also gave specific instructions, as in a letter of 29 September 1827, when at his request Zelter was attending the large scientific meeting in Munich (it reached Zelter only on 21 October). The stay-at-home traveller in Weimar began by saying he was glad to be able again to write to Zelter when he was away from Berlin, as his journeys were "always so fruitful for me." He continued, with regard to the meeting of naturalists:

> First of all, I would like to ask you to give my best greetings to Director von Schelling and to thank him from me for his splendid letter… Then in the friendliest way pass on my respects to Mr. von Martius, the botanist and specialist on Brazil. You will find him to be a truly excellent man. Please ask him to forgive me for my long silence, as I haven't had time to indulge my love for the grandeur of nature, and beseech him for a few lines to me.

Three further instructions regarding specific persons follow, along with a request to pass on greetings to anyone else Goethe might know and, finally, a general exhortation concerning the participating natural scientists:

> Knowing you, you will get on with everyone… Take note of others at this large assembly and tell me who interests you, whether because of his conversation or his lecture. Listen to what they think about each other, whether they get along and to what extent each desires to learn from the others. Listen to what the Protestants and Catholics are saying, too; there are so many kinds of people at the meeting in Munich that a fermentation must take place before this juice is refined into wine.

He closed the letter by urging Zelter to "write a lot and in haste, even if you might at times strike out some words, and send me each page as soon as the ink dries on it."

From Munich on 18 September 1827 Zelter reported:

> The first meeting of the friends of nature took place between 9 and 11 a.m. at the town hall. That I attended you would have found unbelievable, so instead I went to the Glyptothek and looked again at the beautiful antiquities, whose qualities you would certainly appreciate. I did go with the group to dinner, which was not too bad for 36 kreuzer. There were almost 300 persons in one large room, among them Count von Sternberg, Mr. von Cotta and Mr. Froriep. With Cotta I toasted: what we love! The meal was quite lively and amusing. Now I shall go to the theatre to see the famous Mr. Eslair as King Lear, who has always eluded me, without either of us being to blame for it.

Four days later, Zelter described the conference:

> Next year the meeting will be held in Berlin. Humboldt was elected as Director and Lichtenstein as General Secretary. Today the King is expected to attend the meeting and so I will go, too… In the evening: this was the last session, and because of the King I stayed until finally a chamberlain extended to the whole company of naturalists and doctors an invitation to a luncheon banquet. That I don't belong to the group is self-evident, but I found my name on the list and will certainly attend so that I can report to you about the best thing that has happened to us. Good old Röschlaub spoke for a very long time and when I (who can take a lot) say that, you can imagine that everything he said was fairly general and could be understood by any educated person, whether he is a doctor or will become one. But in the end, I have it much too good in this company: I'm not responsible for anything, I enjoy the event along with the others and at every noon meal my neighbour becomes a new friend, maybe even two, at least for the day and the next one. The wine is too sour for me, but the beer is as clear as wine and so good for me that I have not spent anything at all on wine.

The next day, Zelter wrote to Goethe about the invitation to the palace:

> We had been directed to be at the palace at two in the

> afternoon, and I found everyone already at attention. The Minister of the Interior, Count von Armansperg, and some other courtiers received us and greeted especially those of us who were known to them, and soon after that we continued to the dining table which I found very satisfactory, as I was hungry and thirsty... At 3:30 we adjourned to another room for coffee, where the King appeared in uniform, spoke to scholars whom he knew and asked about others. He was especially courteous and pleasant to those who were from out of town... After he had spoken to the men next to me, he said to me What is your name? – Zelter, Your Majesty – I must have spoken too softly and he asked me again, holding his ear toward me: What is your name? – Professor Zelter, from Berlin! – Oh, now I know; you looked familiar to me; did I not see your portrait at Goethe's house in Weimar? – That's very possible, Your Majesty, and a great honour for me. – Quite right, and nicely painted; you have a good friend in Goethe? – I hope I am for him what he is to me. – I was very pleased to see him and I travelled to Weimar for that reason. If I am not mistaken he had already said that to young Buttmann from Berlin, and he added: I am glad to see the gentlemen from Berlin here.

In later letters, Zelter wrote about the remainder of his stay, during which he attended social events and many opera and theatre performances, visited museums and enjoyed becoming acquainted with other attractions in

Munich, such as the extensive park known as the English Garden, because he knew Goethe would like to hear about them. On 27 September 1827 he reported:

> I happened to come into conversation… with Prof. Martius… (who is the Recording Secretary), [he] asked why he didn't have my name in the list of naturalists. – If I had the honour of travelling with two botanists (Lichtenstein and Hayne) to Munich and found here the distinction of acceptance by the most worthy men of our time, then I am at least an amateur naturalist who is delighted to enjoy with the others what they have discovered… By the bye, this Martius is a man whom I like very much…

Goethe's armchair travelling clearly included the decisive element of participation from afar. Nothing better demonstrates this participatory dimension, already on display in his correspondence with other travellers, than his interaction with Zelter's reports. Nonetheless, even though he followed the journeys of his friend intensely by means of letters and subsequent accounts, he remained aware of the differences between Zelter's style of life and his own. The former lived firmly in the worlds of music, architecture and construction, while his own world, as he said on 1 June 1831, was like "living in a monastery garden," where he stayed because he felt impelled to produce as much work as he could during the time remaining to him.

The extent to which Goethe relished Zelter's travel accounts can also be seen in the fact that he wished to share them with others, both in published form and in person. Joseph Sebastian Grüner, for example, an Imperial Austrian municipal officer in Eger with whom Goethe often met when visiting there, noted in 1822 in his diary:

> 6 August, in the evening. At home Goethe conversed at length about musical compositions, especially those of Zelter, his oldest friend, as he called him. You should become acquainted with them, he said, I wish I had such a temperament as his.

Upon which, Grüner reported, Goethe pulled out a piece of paper and read from Zelter's report about his visit to Herrnhut. Grüner continued:

> Even if the letter had been less witty, and less full of droll opinions, just the fact that Goethe was reading it aloud would have charmed us, for he could put himself totally into his friend's train of thought and modulate his voice accordingly; in short, he gave a splendid performance, such as I had never before experienced.[2]

What Goethe read to Grüner may have been what Zelter had written beginning on 26 May 1822, after his arrival in Herrnhut. He had stopped there on his way to Dresden, where he was planning to consult with an elderly scholar, Peter Mortimer, who had written about various church music modes. Before that, Zelter wished to experience the celebration of the feast of Pentecost, or Whitsun, in the community founded in the early 18th century by members of the Moravian Brotherhood with assistance from Count Nikolaus von Zinzendorf. He begins by exclaiming about the journey: "The accursed mail coaches have such low ceilings, that if they had a hole in them one could comfortably observe the surroundings," going on to speculate, "time will tell how I get along here… one is among Christians, after all, even though they might rate themselves in their service of the Lord as seemingly higher than the Lord Himself…"

On Whitsunday, Zelter continues:

> 11 a.m. I have just come from the second sermon of today. I knew all of it, believe I know some of it better, or at least differently, but still – how effective an abstruse character who presents something with passion can be once again became clear to me… Both pastors spoke so skilfully, movingly and freely that belief made itself felt as the heart opened, and had organist Jeschke refrained from his double ornamentations and performed with less flamboyance or none at all on his instrument, which consists of a lot of flue stops and not a single pipe, I would have been completely won over by this feast. The congregation sang the chorale *Come Holy Spirit* thoughtfully; it was reverently pure and uplifting, as it should be…

He goes on to add:

> The appearance of the house of worship surprised

> me. The large hall had been painted chalk white; the windows were draped in white, all the women wore chalk-white clothing and sat in rows next to each other – I felt as if I were among the departed, resurrected, ghastly.

On the Tuesday following Whitsun, Zelter wrote from the town of Bautzen:

> Evening. I ran away. At 11 this morning as I came from the sermon I immediately requested horses, ate a few bites and I arrived here about two hours ago. Let those who can bear it, stay: in the evening they even wanted to give a concert for me. No! I can't do it!

As a result of reading and savouring Zelter's travel accounts, Goethe resolved to publish parts of their correspondence as a kind of continuation of his own autobiographical *Annals*. His associate Johann Peter Eckermann referred to this in his record of a conversation with Goethe on 20 June 1827. According to Eckermann, Goethe remarked that he had been working with his adviser and colleague Friedrich Wilhelm Riemer to read through Zelter's letters, and in the process had come upon "some priceless materials." Continuing, Goethe noted: "Especially the letters he wrote to me from his travels are of great value, for, as an able building contractor and musician, he has the advantage of never lacking for an opinion with regard to things of significance." Among Zelter's letters "of great value," Goethe apparently included one about his friend's dangerous trip in a small boat from the northern German island of Rügen across the Bay of Pomerania to the port of Swinemünde during a raging storm, because he mentioned it in a letter to Zelter of 2 March 1827: "Yesterday evening while editing your letters I was again truly afraid for you when I read about your daring and perilous boat trip to Swinemünde and pondered about it."

In that letter, which Zelter had begun on 31 August and did not finish until after he arrived in Stettin around 13 September 1820, he had explained that to get from Rügen to Stolpe to see his son would take several days if he were to go by land, but if he went by sea, he would get there in one day and save both time and money. But, he added, that was just the ostensible reason for the boat trip, because "in actuality I want to know what it is like to be seasick, and so I want to go to sea." What happened was very different from what Zelter had expected:

> A great honour befell me: with my own eyes I experienced a full-fledged storm at sea and lived through it… I had engaged a boat for the ten miles from Rügen to Swinemünde. I was awakened at 3 a.m. on Saturday, September 2. A police constable and a student from Berlin joined me, and with the two boatmen we climbed into their vessel; at 5:15 the little anchor was raised.

Because they had to sail into the wind, for three hours they made minimal progress away from Rügen. Finally they were able to head out to sea, but it remained very windy. Zelter continued:

> At about 9 a.m. the wind-blown clouds increased and closed over, and by 10 nothing more could be seen of the sun, and the horizon and the grey-green sea were a single mass. The waves coming toward us grew higher and higher, until they washed over us, and one of us was constantly occupied with working to bail out the boat. Finally at six in the evening we glimpsed the shipping road before Swinemünde, recognising it from the masts of the ships lying at anchor there, for due to the high waves and the growing darkness the harbour was not discernible. As I beheld these ships, among them four three-masters, dancing on the waves so that both ends kissed the sea and the waves broke over the masts, the danger my little boat was in became clear, especially since we were still more than two miles away. But now we steered to the right, getting the wind behind us, and you should have seen how the wind took our little sail in its arms and seemed to carry us through the air, so that in less than 30 minutes we were sailing between the ships at anchor. Everyone on them came out on deck and cried a joyous hurrah to us, harmonising nicely with the howling of the wind and the rolling of the waves… In the harbour there was a white barrel and a black one, between which we were to sail, but due to the darkness we didn't see one of them, and so the boat went too far to the left on to the so-called

> Platter, where a 50-foot-wide wave picked us up, and our boat could still have capsized there if I had not laid myself forcefully over the highest part of the deck to hold it down. We had plenty of water in the boat and in our clothes, but we reached the bulwark and clambered out cheerfully and in good health... Of myself I can say that I was not seasick for even a moment and during the entire 13-hour trip I happily gave myself over to the unending movement with which the sea differentiates itself from great flowing waters; the river that runs into the sea appears in comparison to be like a child coming from school, and so I lost all feeling of my own importance, and my whole being was nothing more than eyes and ears. When I think now how a thin piece of wood separated me from the open sea, and how my early death would have caused you and my whole family to go into deep mourning, I shudder, but I don't remember having any such thought at the time.

Immediately after receiving Zelter's letter on 20 September 1820, Goethe had responded to his "wave-rocked, sea air-sniffing, shore-yearning" friend: "This is really something! I left you with the irresistible princess, toasting everyone's health, and now I behold you on an expanse of salty waves about to swallow a horrible swill that could never be used for a toast."

As Goethe prepared the correspondence for publication, on 9 January 1827 he even asked Zelter: "Might you have time to undertake a small trip to anywhere in the world you would like? I felt compelled to make this odd request after Riemer and I were greatly amused while reading your delightful account of your trip to Baden, Vienna, Prague, etc." And Goethe added: "It was clear from this letter that you are never more conversable than when you are on the road." Following this encouragement, Zelter travelled to Munich. It was the last journey that he wrote about to Goethe.

Although Zelter tended in his letters to report on topics he knew would interest Goethe, and even in time adopted some of his friend's thought patterns and writing style, he never wrote a line that was not completely his own. Goethe so thoroughly enjoyed Zelter's descriptions of his adventures that they seemed to serve him as a continuation of his own travels, even though he himself was now content with his stay-at-home life. Perhaps visiting places such as Vienna, Amsterdam and Swinemünde on paper with Zelter was almost like seeing them himself, as had also been the case with Berlin, and he was thus able to regard his friend's letters as a complement to his own writings, as well as an expression of his enjoyable mental travels.

Beyond the Chinese Wall to "World Poetry" and "World Literature"

In contrast to his prolonged occupation with Hafez and immersion in Near Eastern poetry and culture, Goethe's armchair travels to the Far East were of short duration. His diaries record a brief reading focus on Chinese matters in the first half of October 1813, and then again, more than a decade later, a literary journey to China in 1827. These latter readings in Chinese fiction overlap and merge with Goethe's renewed surge of interest for world poetry and his reflections about world literature. Prior to his targeted excursions to the immense land beyond the Great Wall of China, a few noteworthy remarks scattered throughout his works indicate his ongoing awareness and respect for the Chinese cultural tradition.

In the 1797 epigram "Der Chinese in Rom" ("The Chinese Man in Rome"), the writer observes a visitor from China contemplating the massive stone buildings of antiquity and the Renaissance with eyes accustomed to different architectural standards:

> I saw a Chinese man in Rome; all the buildings of
> ancient and modern times seemed cumbersome and

> heavy to him. 'Oh!' he sighed, 'those poor people! I hope they might one day understand how, when slender columns of wood carry the roof canopy, the finer taste of a cultivated eye enjoys the slats and pasteboard, the carvings and the bright gilding.'

The divergent architectural perspective of the Chinese man shows that the aesthetic norms of classical antiquity are relative, as the tourist used to the colourful lightness of decorated Chinese temples finds the heaviness of Roman stone structures unattractive.

And in Goethe's *Italian Journey,* the visitor to the Borgiano Museum in Naples stops to admire two painted Chinese porcelain boxes featuring realistic depictions of silkworm breeding and of rice-field work:

> I noticed two Chinese watercolour boxes, where on the sides of the first one the entire process of raising silkworms was represented, and on the other rice cultivation, both treated quite simply and executed with care. The small boxes and the displays were particularly beautiful.

Rather than the decorative chinoiserie with its lavish display of luxury favoured by the 18th-century rococo style, he finds the representation of the interaction of nature and industriousness depicted on objects of daily life "particularly beautiful." The Chinese porcelain he admired in the Borgiano Museum modelled a different kind of aesthetic, where design and practical function intersect.

On another occasion, during a visit to an exhibition of Raphael's tapestries in the Vatican, he observes that the high-warp method by which they were created was similar to the sophisticated weaving technique of precious Chinese carpets he had seen elsewhere. "All early beginnings of art and technology are of this kind; we have seen beautiful Chinese carpets that were executed in the same fashion." Piercing beneath the surface, his sharp visual perception senses that in the encounter with Chinese civilisation, Europeans may need to be the students rather than the teachers.

Chinese Readings

"Sinica" is the Latin designation used in Goethe's diaries for his Chinese travels of October 1813. Starting with the well-known *Reise in den Orient während der Jahre 1272 bis 1295*[1] (*Travels to the Orient during the Years 1272 to 1295*) by the Venetian merchant-explorer Marco Polo, the most famous early traveller to Central and East Asia, his readings included philosophical, historical and geographical accounts by Jesuit missionaries; by the Dutch Enlightenment philosopher Jan Cornelis de Pauw, who rejected the popular theory that China was originally a colony of Ancient Egypt; by the English traders Sir George Thomas Staunton and Sir John Barrow; and by Chrétien-Louis-Joseph de Guignes, a French Sinologist who spent 17 years in China, and came back to publish in 1808 the three-volume *Voyages à Péking, Manille et l'Île de France*[2] (*Voyages to Peking, Manilla and the Island of Mauritius*).

During the same period, Goethe also interacted with the German linguist, explorer and cartographer Julius Heinrich Klaproth, who had travelled to the Caucasus and the Russian–Chinese border and could discuss with him the geology of Central Asia.

Goethe's statement in his 10 November 1813 letter to his friend Carl Ludwig von Knebel explaining his surge of interest in the Far East would be echoed shortly afterward in connection with his Persian hegira: "I had set aside and sequestered, so to speak, that important country [China], in order to flee there in case of need, as has now happened. To find one's self in a completely new situation, even if only in spirit, is very therapeutic."

The comment indicates that his interest was not new, since he had already kept China in his thoughts as a country "of importance." A later remark in the *Annals for the Year 1813* is more explicit about what he meant by the need to escape his surroundings: "When something tremendously threatening emerged in the political world, I flung myself stubbornly in the furthest removed direction."

An immediate incentive for an escape was the Battle of Nations of 16 to 19 October 1813 at Leipzig that ushered in the downfall of Napoleon's empire and brought military confrontations all the way to Goethe's doorstep in Weimar. The same response that had transported him to the "furthest removed" regions of the world was soon redirected by his new fascination with the Middle East and Hafez' poetry, which became his main creative involvement in the following years.

A decade later Goethe returned to China, this time with

a new emphasis on Chinese fiction and poetry, which he read in German translations from the English and the French. The Parisian literary journal *Le Globe*, of which he was a faithful and engaged reader in his later years, had played a role in rekindling his interest. On 28 October 1826 it announced the publication of the translated Chinese novel *Iu-Kiao-Li* (*The Two Fair Cousins*), describing it as a literary journey into the unknown world of Chinese society. A review of the French translation by Jean-Pierre Abel-Rémusat who held the first Chair of Sinology at the Collège de France in Paris, followed in December.

In 1827, Goethe recorded in his diaries his reading of several books of Chinese fiction in translation: in February, the verse novel *Huajian ji*, or *Chinese Courtship* in an English translation by Peter Perring Thoms of the East India Company; in May, Abel-Rémusat's French translation of *Iu-Kiao-Li, ou les Deux Cousines*; and in August, the *Contes chinois* (*Chinese Tales*), also published by Abel-Rémusat.[3]

An addendum to *Chinese Courtship*, called "The Songs of a Hundred Fine Women," included poems about famous female poets that inspired him to try out his own adaptations based on them for his periodical *On Art and Antiquity*. A conversation reported by Eckermann on 31 January 1827 also highlights Goethe's appreciation for China's centuries-long literary tradition: the Chinese had "thousands of novels," he remarked, at a time when "our ancestors still lived in the woods"; and underscoring his interest in cross-cultural similarities across the cultural divide, he added: "[Chinese] people think, act and feel almost the same as we do, and one soon feels as if one were among peers."

In contrast to this focus on universal human traits, Goethe's poetic adaptations from *Chinese Courtship* in four short pieces titled "Chinesisches" ("Chinese Topics"), deal with typically Chinese customs. One of the poems, which centres on female foot binding, sublimates the gruesome practice into the aesthetic picture of a lotus-footed dancer floating on water lilies. According to the translator's commentary, the dancer's female companions in the harem were so envious of her tiny feet that they began to bind their own feet in order to emulate her. From that point on, "so the story goes," the custom "spread to the entire nation." The poet joins the English translator, albeit with reservations, in deflecting the shocking effect of the cruel practice by placing the burden of its origin on female rivalry.

Fräulein See-Yeaou-Hing	Miss See-Yeaou-Hing
Du tanzest leicht bey Pfirsich-Flor	You dance so lightly among the peach blossoms
Am luftigen Frühlings-Ort:	In the breezy spring orchard:
Der Wind, stellt man den Schirm nicht vor,	Without the umbrella's shade
Bläst euch zusammen fort.	The wind will blow you away.
Auf Wasserlilien hüpftest du	You frolic on water lilies

Wohl hin den bunten Teich,	Flitting around the bright pond,
Dein winziger Fuss, dein zarter Schuh	Your tiny foot, your dainty shoe
Sind selbst der Lilie gleich.	Themselves look like the lilies.
Die andern binden Fuss fuer Fuss,	The others bind foot after foot,
Und wenn sie ruhig stehn	And when they quietly stand
Gelingt wohl noch ein holder Gruss,	They still can bow,
Doch können sie nicht gehn.	But cannot manage to walk.

As was the case with his poetic variations on Persian poetry, Goethe's adaptations from translated Chinese sources proceeded from textual imitations to free compositions. The most sophisticated poetic testimonial to his literary voyages to China, *Chinesisch-deutsche Jahres- und Tageszeiten* (*Chinese–German Book of Seasons and Hours*), a lyrical cycle in 14 stanzas, was composed in 1827 and first published in 1830. The title has its direct precedent in the intercultural heading of the *West-East Divan*. While the text itself cannot be traced back to identifiable sources, its minimalist composition style shows the influence of Chinese poetic techniques, and its blend of natural and ethical themes comes close to Chinese concepts of nature. The poet's "alter ego" is an old mandarin, a court official "tired of governing and serving" who retires into his lakeside garden to meditate, drink and write. The seasonal cycle and the hours of the days float in front of his eyes in a changing sequence of images of nature depicted with the stylised brush strokes of Chinese watercolour paintings: white lilies with reddish edges, lanes lined with spring daffodils, green meadows, sunshine lifting a veil of fog, a shrieking peacock, radiant evening sun spying on lovers, a house roof and fence hidden behind summer growth, memories of meeting a lover in the open, twilight falling on the lake, the moon flickering through the willows and a cool breeze calming the heart. Observations merge with mental associations, fixating on a last rosebud glowing past its time on a stem as an immanent symbol of the "eternal law that makes the rose and the lily blossom." Gradually, the poet turns his imagery into a vivid illustration of his theory of plant metamorphosis that hints at the affinity between his own philosophy of nature and Chinese concepts of the natural world, concluding with a practical, Confucian exhortation to avoid daydreaming and to focus on the duties of the day. Much as had been the case with the *West-East Divan*, however, which had met with only a tepid reception, the intercultural mode of Goethe's *Chinese–German Book of Seasons and Hours* was not to the taste of his 19th-century contemporaries and had to wait for some years to be accorded the appreciation that it deserved.

World Poetry

While Goethe's concept of "World Literature" is connected to a modern process of globalisation that he was witnessing in his late years, his lifelong interest in the manifestations of folk poetry in various languages and countries is oriented to the early stages of human culture. "World poetry," he noted in his periodical *On Art and Antiquity*, is a worldwide gift that emerges spontaneously anywhere, "wherever the sun shines." World poetry knows no national identity and no borders, yet it stems from a specific culture and language. Where world literature is the product of international exchange, world poetry is regional and local. Like Alexander von Humboldt's vegetal kingdom, its home is the environment from which it stems. During his time as a student in Strasbourg, Goethe's friend Johann Gottfried Herder had directed his attention to Celtic and northern European folk poetry, as well as to the older folk songs of the Alsace region. Throughout his long career, folk poetry from a variety of cultures continued to nourish Goethe's own poetic expression. In the 1820s, his role as a promoter of world poetry was intensified by his imaginary voyages to the Orient, to the Far East and to the Americas. His preoccupation with the worldwide prevalence of poetry in his later years also functioned as a counterpoint to the exclusivity of national poetry cultivated in the Romantic age, especially in Germany.

In 1823 and 1824, *On Art and Antiquity* included and discussed translated Serbian folk songs, which recently had been taken up by several collectors and German translators, and in 1826 Goethe included in his periodical a short Brazilian poem as an example of world poetry. It was his more recent adaptation of a love song he had first published in 1782 under the title "Liebeslied eines amerikanischen Wilden" ("Love Song of an American Savage"), which had originally appeared much earlier in the essay "Of Cannibals" by the French Renaissance author Michel de Montaigne.

Brasilianisch	***Brazilian Motif***
Schlange, halte stille!	Snake, hold still!
Halte stille, Schlange!	Hold still, snake!
Meine Schwester will von dir ab	My sister would like
Sich ein Muster nehmen;	To use you as a pattern
Sie will eine Schnur mir flechten,	She wants to plait me a belt
Reich und bunt wie du bist,	As rich and colourful as you are
Dass ich sie der Liebsten schenke.	To give to my sweetheart.
Trägt sie die, so wirst du	Whenever she wears it,
Immerfort von allen Schlangen	You will forever be praised
Herrlich schön gepriesen.	As the loveliest among all snakes.

To underscore the direct connection between humans and the natural world that is the hallmark of world poetry, Goethe's newer version of the poem focuses on the colourful pattern of the snakeskin braided into a decorative belt. It is conceivable that Goethe may have been reminded of his earlier adaptation while he was studying the snake watercolours of Maximilian zu Wied-Neuwied, published after the explorer's return from Brazil.

Looking back at the centuries-long tradition of Chinese poetry, Goethe repeated in a 31 January 1827 discussion with Eckermann his belief that "poetry is a common good of humanity which manifests itself everywhere and in all times in hundreds and hundreds of people."

After translating several Serbian folk songs for *On Art and Antiquity*, Goethe composed an exuberant panegyric on world poetry, calling it "a gift of the nations of the world":

Wie David königlich zur Harfe sang,	As royally as David sang on his harp,
Der Winzerin Lied am Throne lieblich klang,	As sweet as the vintner maiden's song rang by the throne,
Des Persers Bulbul Rosenbusch umbangt,	As the Persian thrush yearns for the rose bush,
Und Schlangenhaut als Wildengürtel prangt,	And snakeskin glistens on the native's belt,
Von Pol zu Pol Gesänge sich erneun –	Songs are renewed from pole to pole
Ein Sphärentanz harmonisch im Getümmel –	A celestial harmony in the tumult of the world

Lasst alle Völker unter gleichem Himmel Sich gleicher Gabe wohlgemuth erfreun!	May all people under the same sky Enjoy the same gift with equal joy!

Linking together ancient poetry from Eastern and Western provenances, from King David's hymns, the Song of Songs and Persian poetry to the native Brazilian's snake belt song, the verses underlined Goethe's belief that world poetry was the manifestation of a natural human faculty, both diverse and universal. As a human music of the soul ringing "from pole to pole," world poetry found its favourite and most perennial expression in the realm of love, and lent inspiration to the sophistication of modern poetry, including Goethe and Marianne von Willemer's "Book of Zuleika."

World Literature

The distance and even animosity clouding Goethe's relations with his late-Romantic contemporaries was not shared abroad, where his translated works were received with enthusiasm by European and North American contemporary authors. Aided by the detailed reviews of European literature published in the French journal *Le Globe* and the British *Foreign Review* and *Foreign Quarterly Review*, he was exposed to and regularly corresponded with writers in other countries. His own journal *On Art and Antiquity* became an important forum dedicated to the promotion and appreciation of international literature, and his elaboration of his own concept of "world literature" grew out of that context of mutual literary exchange.

What Goethe's reflections named "world literature" was neither a normative nor an additive concept, for it did not mean "the best works" or "all the works of literature" as in the current pedagogical use of the concept. It denoted an interactive process of international communication and dialogue, conveyed through the medium of literature. World poetry is both the polar opposite and the complement of world literature, for both concepts can work hand in hand, just as Goethe's appreciation of ancient poetry from various parts of the world and his lively personal interaction with writers and translators from other countries complemented each other.

Translations of important literary works played a key role in such international literary exchange, as illustrated by the activity of what had been the Society for German Literature in Berlin. On the occasion of Goethe's birthday on 28 August 1829, it became the Berlin Society for Foreign Literature, expanding its reach to European literature with the goal of promoting understanding through sharing and publishing literary creations across language borders.

Goethe wholeheartedly endorsed the new international mission of the society. In that context, he found a most engaged and congenial peer in the translator of his *Wilhelm Meister* novels, the Scottish historian Thomas Carlyle, who had also written *The Life of Friedrich Schiller* and compiled a four-volume anthology of translated German short stories and fairy tales titled *German*

Romance.[4] Except for a planned but never completed essay on world literature, the lengthy introduction that Goethe contributed to *Leben Schillers*,[5] the German version of Carlyle's *The Life of Friedrich Schiller*, conveys the most elaborate formulation of his concept of world literature:

> For some time already, the idea of a universal world literature has become a subject of discussion, and not without reason: for all the nations, shaken into chaos by the most terrible wars, once brought back to their own individual status realised that they had become aware of some things that had been foreign to them, had absorbed them and had felt here and there intellectual needs that previously were unknown to them. This gave rise to a sensitivity for neighbourly relations and, instead of closing themselves off, as had been the case before, they began to develop a desire to be involved in more or less free intellectual exchanges.

His own interaction with Carlyle was a prime example of the "intellectual exchanges" envisioned in Goethe's idea of world literature. In that spirit and to that end, he nominated Carlyle to become a member of the Berlin Society for Foreign Literature. He also recommended to the Society the German translation of the lyrics of the Romantic Scottish poet Robert Burns, whose life and works he had also celebrated in his introduction to *Leben Schillers*. World literature, as understood by Goethe, was a dynamic process in which not only the reading and review of literary works, but also personal and literary connections across language and cultural borders reinforced and enhanced each other.

In order to help readers feel a closer personal connection to Carlyle, Goethe's introduction to *Leben Schillers* also included his Scottish collaborator's own description of the surroundings of the country home in Craigenputtock in the district of Dumfries to which he had retired. To visualise and reinforce the effect of Carlyle's description, the frontispiece of the German edition of Carlyle's *The Life of Friedrich Schiller* featured a lithograph of his Scottish residence and its surroundings (see Figure 16).

As affirmed in Goethe's introduction to Carlyle's biography of Schiller, world literature does not exhaust itself in the exercise of mutual intellectual appreciation. It is an attitude of intercultural openness that can act as a contribution to international peace in a world long ravaged by the horrors of war. To underscore the hope for a peaceful impact of intercultural understanding fostered through the medium of literature, which was also part and parcel of his concept of world literature, Goethe's introduction to the Schiller biography concluded by quoting a simple but powerful wish expressed in a letter from Carlyle of 22 December 1829 that still resonates for us today: "Simply let nations and individuals get to know each other, and their mutual hatred will turn into mutual assistance; and instead of natural enemies, as neighbouring countries are often called, we shall all become natural friends."

The Last Trip to Italy

Like many learned Europeans since the Renaissance, Goethe's father Johann Caspar made a cultural pilgrimage to Italy, which he memorialised in the architectural engravings that he hung around the upper landing of his Frankfurt house. His son Johann Wolfgang grew up amidst these venerable antiquities, dreaming of travelling to the southern land of art and nature, which he finally achieved after his busy first decade in Weimar. To follow in his father's and grandfather's footsteps and travel to Italy was also the cherished wish of Johann Wolfgang's son, August – yet, rather than helping him forge a pathway to self-sufficiency, August's own Italian journey, taken up under the long shadow of his overpowering father, ended in tragedy. Ten days after his arrival in Rome, August von Goethe died of a stroke at the untimely age of 40. The autopsy linked his death to a meningitis attack compounded by long-standing alcoholic excess.

Grandfather, father and son each left behind a narrative account of their respective trips to Italy: Johann Caspar Goethe's *Viaggio in Italia*, Johann Wolfgang Goethe's own monumental *Italian Journey* and August von Goethe's travel diaries. Starting in Frankfurt, and with stations in Milan, Venice, Genoa, La Spezia, Florence and Naples before ending in Rome, where he arrived on 16 October, August's travel narratives form the bulk of the correspondence he sent to Weimar at regular intervals during the six months of his Italian journey. They have since been published as *Auf einer Reise nach Süden: Tagebuch 1830*[1] (*On a Journey to the South: Diaries 1830*).

During his short life, August faithfully performed administrative duties, both as court chamberlain and as his father's confidant, mediator and business, legal and social assistant, but he was never able to free himself from the strictures of filial responsibilities. His marriage to Ottilie von Pogwisch also suffered from the burden of his dependency. The story of his Italian diaries provides a telling example of the predicament. The elder Goethe, for whom living and writing were intimately intertwined, always placed the highest priority on transmitting his lived experiences to paper, especially when he found himself immersed in new surroundings. He urged those around him – not only friends and associates like Carl Friedrich Zelter and Johann Peter Eckermann, but also his own son, August – to keep travel diaries. Thus the motive for August's narrative of his trip to Italy, and also its outcome, could hardly have been more starkly different from those of the travels of his father's contemporaries, which fed Goethe's unquenchable thirst for new experience and knowledge. It was his interest for novelty and his search for escape that attracted him to Hammer-Purgstall's translations of Hafez' poetry; scientific and exotic discovery that fascinated him in Alexander von

Humboldt's travel writings; factual eyewitness reports that he appreciated in Duke Bernhard's North American journals; and Zelter's gift for entertaining descriptions and anecdotes that made his trip reports so enjoyable. In the case of August, who was following a travel route familiar to his father, the written outcome was preordained by paternal intent. August was, one might say, charged with being an on-site reporter from the Italian peninsula, whose duty was to report as faithfully as possible the details of his journey. His trip diaries, undertaken at his father's wish, were weighed down in no small part by pedagogical purposefulness.

It would hardly be an overstatement to say that his travelogue came about because of his father's insistence on its importance as the "chief goal" of August's trip to Italy. In his letters to his son, Goethe often mentioned the diaries as one of the most significant products of August's travels, projecting onto the son his own obsession for the transformation of the experiential into literary form. Contrary to his own advice that August should always search for the new and unexpected, such as "visiting sites, that you have never seen," at times he dictated specifically what his son should do or see. After August left Milan with his travelling companion Eckermann, his father wrote: "We will soon hear of your wanderings through Lombardy." Later on, looking forward to August's arrival in Rome, Goethe instructed him in no uncertain terms that he expected to read about his "entry through the Porta del Popolo." In August's reaction to Rome the father expected to hear an echo of his own youthful enthusiasm, writing on 3 September to his son: "Whoever has entered Rome" feels that he is "born again!"

Due to the slow pace of postal coaches, there was a long gap between August's death on the night of 26 to 27 October 1830 and Goethe's receipt of the tragic news on the evening of 10 November. Goethe's last letter to his son, dictated between 8 and 10 November, was left unfinished. Its tone of cheerful expectation clashes with the reality of August's hectic days in Rome, where he was hosted by German artists. The son's Roman diary leaves the impression of an intense effort to put into writing the busy sightseeing schedule of that last, fateful week, which even included a commemorative visit to the Campagna, the site of Tischbein's 1787 painting *Goethe in the Roman Campagna*.

August von Goethe was buried in the *Cimitero Acattolico* (Cemetery for Non-Catholics) of Rome, not far from the pyramid of the Roman tribune Caius Cestius. The burial site was eerily predicted in the *Italian Journey*, where Goethe declared that he would like to have his eternal resting place located near the Cestius pyramid in Rome. Faced with the funerary monument, the visitor to the cemetery will look in vain for much information about the deceased. Neither August's full name nor his dates of birth and death are inscribed on the tall tombstone, a fact that has been rightfully bemoaned by critics. Instead, there is a Latin inscription, composed by Goethe at the behest of the German artists in Rome:

GOETHE FILIVS	GOETHE'S SON,
PATRI	PRECEDING
ANTEVERTENS	HIS FATHER,
OBIIT	DIED
ANNOR XL	AT THE AGE OF 40
MDCCCXXX	IN 1830

In a cruel irony, August entered Rome not to find himself "born again," but to suffer a fateful death and a burial where his father himself had wished to be interred. At that sad juncture near the end of Goethe's lifetime, the armchair travels he had enjoyed for so long, and from which his own work had steadily profited, took a final turn to sorrow.

Acknowledgements

This book would not have been written were it not for the interest of Barbara Schwepcke, owner of Haus Publishing, in an in-depth exploration of Goethe's role as an armchair traveller. The last stages of the manuscript composition have benefitted from her seasoned editorial advice, and from the tireless input and dedication of Jo Stimpson, editor and project manager at Haus Publishing. The authors want to express their gratitude to both for their careful oversight of the project. We are also grateful for ongoing access to the extensive library collections of Indiana University Bloomington, and for the librarians who have assisted our searches with patience and determination. Our special thanks go not only to Teodora Durbin, Interlibrary Loan Librarian at Indiana University-Purdue University Indianapolis, but to the experts who have guided us to the sources of illustrative materials and/or lent us permission to reproduce them. Among these committed and generous professionals we owe our deepest gratitude to Erica Dowell, Associate Director and Curator of Modern Books and Manuscripts at the Lilly Library, Bloomington, and Joachim Seng, Director of the Library of the Goethe-Haus, Frankfurt.

Notes

Most passages quoted from Goethe's diaries and letters are identified by the date of their writing. All were drawn and translated from parts III and IV of the first and still most comprehensive historical–critical edition of Goethe's works, the Weimarer Ausgabe [WA], or Weimar edition, in 143 volumes, published under the aegis of Princess Sophie of Sachsen-Weimar (Weimar: Hermann Böhlau, 1887–1919). The monumental Weimar edition is also available as a reprint (München: Deutscher Taschenbuch Verlag, 1987–90) and in digital form (*Goethes Werke Im WWW*, Cambridge, UK: Chadwyck-Healey, 1997, https://goethe.chadwyck.com/), available in a number of libraries throughout the world.

Passages from Goethe's literary and scientific works are drawn and translated from the 40-volume Frankfurter Ausgabe (Frankfurt edition) of *Johann Wolfgang Goethe, Sämtliche Werke. Briefe, Tagebücher und Gespräche* (*Johann Wolfgang Goethe, Complete Works. Letters, Diaries and Conversations*), eds. Friedmar Apel, Hendrik Birus, Anne Bohnenkamp et al. (Frankfurt a.M.: Deutscher Klassiker Verlag, 1987–2013).

Passages from conversations between Goethe and his assistant Johann Peter Eckermann, subsequently recorded by Eckermann, are identified by date and translated from his *Gespräche mit Goethe in den letzten Jahren seines Lebens* (*Conversations with Goethe in the Last Years of His Life*), ed. Heinz Schlaffer, which comprises vol. 19 in *Johann Wolfgang Goethe, Sämtliche Werke nach Epochen seines Schaffens – Münchner Ausgabe* (*Goethe's Complete Works in Chronological Stages of Their Creation – Munich Edition*), ed. Karl Richter et al. (München: Hanser, 1985–98).

Passages quoted from Goethe's correspondence with Wilhelm and Alexander von Humboldt are translated from *Goethes Briefwechsel mit Wilhelm und Alexander von Humboldt* (*Goethe's Correspondence with Wilhelm and Alexander von Humboldt*), ed. Ludwig Geiger (Berlin: Hans Bondy, 1909).

Passages quoted from the voluminous correspondence between Goethe and his Berlin friend Carl Friedrich Zelter are identified by the date of their writing and translated from *Briefwechsel zwischen Goethe und Zelter in den Jahren 1799 bis 1832* (*Correspondence between Goethe and Zelter in the Years from 1799 to 1832*), eds. Hans-Günter Ottenberg and Edith Zehm et al., which comprises vols. 20.1–20.3 of the Munich edition.

All of the quotations from the journals of Duke Bernhard of Sachsen-Weimar-Eisenach are translated from *Reise Sr. Hoheit des Herzogs Bernhard zu Sachsen-Weimar-Eisenach durch Nord-Amerika in den Jahren 1825 und 1826* (*Travels of His Highness Duke Bernhard of Sachsen-Weimar-Eisenach through North America in the Years 1825 and 1826*), ed. Heinrich Luden. 2 vols. (Weimar: Wilhelm Hoffmann, 1828).

Passages from Goethe's correspondence with his son August are translated from *Goethes Briefwechsel mit seinem Sohn August*, ed. Gerlinde Ulm Sanford. 2 vols. (Weimar: Böhlau, 2005).

All translations stem from the authors of this volume with the exception of several poems from Goethe's *West-East Divan* (see note 1 in the chapter "Goethe's Poetic Journey to the Orient").

The description of Figures 7, 8 and 9 in the chapter "To Latin America with Humboldt" is based on Gabrielle Bersier's discussion of those three images in "Picturing the Physiognomy of the Equinoctial Landscape: Goethe and Alexander von Humboldt's 'Ideen zu einer Geographie der Pflanzen'", pp. 344–351 in *Forster – Humboldt – Chamisso: Weltreisende im Spannungsfeld der Kulturen*, ed. Julian Drews, Ottmar Ette, Tobias Kraft, Barbara Schneider-Kempf and Julia Weber (Göttingen: Vanderhoeck & Ruprecht unipress, 2017).

Introduction

1. George Anson Anson, Baron, Richard Walter and Benjamin Robins, *A Voyage Round the World in the Years MDCCXL, I, II, III, IV,* 2d ed. (London: John and Paul Knapton, 1748). A more recent edition is *A Voyage round the World, in the Years MDCCXL, I, II, III, IV: Compiled from papers and Other Materials of the Right Honourable George Lord Anson, and published under His Direction, by Richard*

Walter, Chaplain to His Majesty's Ship the Centurion (Cambridge: Cambridge University Press, 2014).
2. Hans Ruppert, *Goethes Bibliothek: Katalog* (Weimar: Arion, 1958).
3. Elise von Keudell, *Goethe als Benutzer der Weimarer Bibliothek. Ein Verzeichnis der von ihm entliehenen Werke* (Weimar: Hermann Böhlaus Nachfolger, 1931).
4. Johann Jacob Volkmann, *Historisch-kritische Nachrichten von Italien, welche eine genaue Beschreibung dieses Landes, der Sitten und Gebräuche... enthalten. Aus den neuesten französischen und englischen Reisebeschreibungen und aus eignen Anmerkungen zusammengetragen*. 3 vols. (Leipzig: C. Fritsch, 1770–71).
5. Volkmann, vol. 3, p. 146.

Journeys to England

1. Karl Philipp Moritz, *Reisen eines Deutschen in England im Jahr 1782* (Berlin: Friedrich Maurer, 1783).
2. Thomas Carlyle, *The Life of Friedrich Schiller: Comprehending an Examination of His Works* (London: Taylor and Hessey, 1825). Multiple subsequent editions.
3. Philipp Andreas Nemnich, *Neueste Reise durch England, Schottland und Ireland, hauptsächlich in bezug auf Produkte, Fabriken und Handlung* (Tübingen: J.G. Cotta, 1807).

4. Charles Dupin, *Voyages dans la Grande-Bretagne, entrepris relativement aux services publics de la guerre, de la marine, et des ponts et chaussées, au commerce et à l'industrie, depuis 1816*. 4 vols. (Paris: Bachelier, 1820–24).
5. Heinrich Meidinger, *Reisen durch Großbritannien und Irland vorzüglich in topographischer, kommerzieller und statistischer Hinsicht: Neuestes Handbuch für Reisende durch die drei vereinigten Königreiche England, Schottland und Irland*. 2 vols. (Frankfurt a.M.: H.L. Brönner, 1828).
6. Johanna Schopenhauer, *Erinnerungen von einer Reise in den Jahren 1803, 1804 und 1805*. 3 vols. (Rudolstadt: Im Verlage der Hof-Buch-und-Kunsthandlung, 1813–17).
7. Hermann Fürst von Pückler-Muskau, *Briefe eines Verstorbenen: Ein fragmentarisches Tagebuch aus England, Wales, Irland und Frankreich, geschrieben in den Jahren 1826–29*. 2 vols. (Stuttgart: Hallberger, 1831).
8. George Greenough, *A Critical Examination of the First Principles of Geology in a Series of Essays* (London: Longman, Hurst, Rees, Orme, and Brown, 1819).
9. Thomas Birch, *The History of the Royal Society of London for Improving of Natural Knowledge, from its First Rise: In Which the Most Considerable of Those Papers Communicated to the Society, Which Have Hitherto Not Been Published, Are Inserted in Their*

Proper Order, as a Supplement to the "Philosophical Transactions." 4 vols. (London: A. Millar, 1756–57).

10. Johann Caspar Lavater, *Physiognomische Fragmente zur Beförderung der Menschenkenntniß und Menschenliebe*. 4 vols. (Leipzig; Winterthur: Bei Weidmanns Erben; Reich; Heinrich Steiner und Compagnie, 1775–78).
11. Anne-Louise-Germaine de Staël-Holstein, *De l'Allemagne*. 3 vols. (Paris: H. Nicolle, 1810). All but four copies of the 10,000-copy first edition were seized and destroyed by the Napoleonic regime. A second edition was published in Paris and Leipzig by Brockhaus in 1814; since then multiple editions in French, German, English and other languages.

Goethe's Poetic Journey to the Orient

1. This and other poems from Goethe's *West-East Divan* are based on Martin Bidney's English rendering of them in his *West-East Divan: The Poems with "Notes and Essays": Goethe's Intercultural Dialogues* (Binghamton, NY: Global Academic Pub., 2010).
2. *Der Diwan von Mohammed Schemsed-din Hafis, aus dem Persischen zum erstenmal ganz übersetzt von Joseph von Hammer*. 2 vols. (Stuttgart; Tübingen: J.G. Cotta, 1812–13).
3. Edward W. Said, *Orientalism* [with a new preface by the author]. 25th Anniversary ed. (New York: Vintage Books, 2003).

4. *Fundgruben des Orients, bearbeitet durch eine Gesellschaft von Liebhabern*, ed. Joseph Freiherr von Hammer-Purgstall. 6 vols. (Vienna: Anton Schmid, 1809–18); Joseph von Hammer-Purgstall, *Geschichte der schönen Redekünste Persiens, mit einer Blüthenlese aus 200 persischen Dichtern* (Vienna: Heubner and Volke, 1818).
5. *Buch des Kabus oder Lehren des persischen Königs Kjekjawus für seinen Sohn Ghilan Schach*, transl. Heinrich Friedrich von Diez (Berlin: Nicolai, 1811); *Denkwürdigkeiten von Asien in Künsten und Wissenschaften, Sitten, Gebräuchen und Alterthümern, Religion und Regierungsverfassung*, ed. H.F. von Diez (Berlin: Nicolai, 1811).
6. Petri della Valle, *Eines vornehmen Römischen Patritii Reiß-Beschreibung in unterschiedliche Theile der Welt* (Geneva: Johann-Herman Widerhold, 1674); Adam Olearius, *Des Welt-berühmten Adami Olearii colligirte und viel vermehrte Reise-Beschreibungen* (Hamburg: Herteln and von Wiering, 1696); Jean-Baptiste Tavernier, *Les six Voyages de Jean-Baptiste Tavernier, Ecuyer Baron d'Aubonne, en Turquie, en Perse, et aux Indes* (Utrecht: Guillaume vande Water; Guillaume & Jacob Poolsum, 1712); Jean Chardin, *Voyages du Chevalier Chardin, en Perse, et autres lieux de l'Orient* (Amsterdam: La Companie, 1735); Carsten Niebuhr, *Beschreibung von Arabien. Aus eigenen Beobachtungen und im Lande selbst gesammelten Nachrichten* (Copenhagen: Nicolaus Möller, 1772).

To Latin America with Alexander von Humboldt

1. Georg Forster, *A Voyage Round the World in His Britannic Majesty's Sloop, Resolution, Commanded by Capt. James Cook, During the Years 1772, 3, 4, and 5.* 2 vols. (London: B. White, J. Robson, P. Elmsly and G. Robinson, 1777); *Reise um die Welt während den Jahren 1772 bis 1775*, transl. Johann Reinhold Forster. 2 vols. (Berlin: Haude und Spener, 1778–80).
2. *Goethes Briefwechsel mit Wilhelm und Alexander von Humboldt*, ed. Ludwig Geiger (Berlin: Hans Bondy, 1909).
3. A. von Humboldt, *Vues des Cordillères et monumens des peuples indigènes de l'Amérique* (Paris: Schoell, (1810–1813).
4. A. de Humboldt, *Relation historique du Voyage aux régions équinoxiales du Nouveau Continent.* 3 vols. (Paris: Schoell, Maze, Smith & Gide, 1814–31).
5. A. de Humboldt, *Essai politique sur l'île de Cuba.* 2 vols. (Paris: Gide, 1826).
6. A. de Humboldt, *Fragmens de géologie et de climatologie asiatiques.* 2 vols. (Paris: Gide, 1831).
7. A. de Humboldt, "Sur les lois que l'on observe dans la distribution des formes végétales," *Annales de chimie et de physique*, March 1816, p. 225–39.
8. A. v. Humboldt, *Ueber den Bau und die Wirkungsart der Vulcane in verschiedenen Erdstrichen* (Berlin: Krause, 1823).

Brazilian Treasures

1. John Mawe, *A Treatise on Diamonds and Precious Stones* (London: Longman, Hurst, Rees, Orme and Brown, 1815); *Travels in the Interior of Brazil, Particularly in the Gold and Diamond Districts of that Country, by Authority of the Prince Regent of Portugal: Including a Voyage to the Rio de la Plata, and an Historical Sketch of the Revolution of Buenos Ayres* (London: Longman, Hurst, Rees, Orme and Brown, 1812).
2. Wilhelm Ludwig von Eschwege, *Journal von Brasilien, oder vermischte Nachrichten aus Brasilien, auf wissenschaftlichen Reisen gesammelt.* 2 vols. (Weimar: Landes-Industrie-Comptoir, 1818).
3. W. von Eschwege, *Geognostisches Gemälde von Brasilien und wahrscheinliches Muttergestein der Diamanten* (Weimar: Landes-Industrie-Comptoir, 1822).
4. Maximilian Prinz zu Wied-Neuwied, *Reise nach Brasilien in den Jahren 1815 bis 1817*, ed. Matthias Glaubrecht (Berlin: Die Andere Bibliothek, 2015). Original edition: Frankfurt a.M. 1820–21.
5. Wied-Neuwied, *Abbildungen zur Naturgeschichte Brasiliens* (Weimar: Landes-Industrie-Comptoir, 1822).
6. Maximilian Prinz zu Wied-Neuwied, *Travels in Brazil in the Years 1815, 1816, 1817* (London: Henry Colburn & Co., 1820), p. 29.

7. Kaspar Maria von Sternberg, *Versuch einer geognostisch-botanischen Darstellung der Flora der Vorwelt*. 2 vols. (Regensburg; Prag: Witwe, 1825–33).
8. Carl Friedrich Philipp von Martius, *Historia Naturalis Palmarum*. 3 vols. (Munich; Leipzig, Auctor; Fleischer; Wolf 1823–50); *Nova Genera et Species Plantarum quas in itinere per Brasiliam annis MDCCCXVII-MDCCCXX* (München: vol. 1, Lindauer, 1824; vols. 2–3, Wolf, 1826–30); Johann Baptist von Spix and Carl Friedrich Philipp von Martius, *Reise in Brasilien in den Jahren 1817 bis 1820*. 3 vols. (Munich: Lindauer, Lentner, Fleischer, 1823, 1828, 1831).
9. C.F.P. von Martius, August Wilhelm Eichler, Ignaz Urban et al., *Flora Brasiliensis: enumeratio plantarum in Brasilia hactenus detectarum quas suis aliorumque botanicorum studiis descriptas et methodo naturali digestas partim icone illustratas*. 15 vols. (Munich; Leipzig: R. Oldenburg; Fleischer, 1840–1906).
10. C.F.P. von Martius, *Die Physiognomie des Pflanzenreiches in Brasilien* (Munich: Lindauer, 1824).

To North America with Duke Bernhard of Sachsen-Weimar-Eisenach

1. D.B. Warden, *Statistical, Political, and Historical Account of the United States of North America*. 3 vols. (Edinburgh: Constable and co., 1819).

2. Parker Cleaveland, *An Elementary Treatise on Mineralogy and Geology… in The United States of America* (Boston: Cummings and Hilliard, 1816).
3. Daniel Fenning, *Neue Erdbeschreibung von ganz Amerika. Dritter Teil* (Göttingen; Leipzig: Weygand, 1777).
4. Daniel Fenning, *A New System of Geography: or, A General Description of the World: Containing a Particular and Circumstantial Account of all the Countries, Kingdoms, and States of Europe, Asia, Africa, and America….* 2 vols. (London: S. Crowder, 1764–65).
5. Karl Bernhard, Duke of Saxe-Weimar-Eisenach, *Travels through North America, During the Years 1825 and 1826 by His Highness, Bernhard, Duke of Saxe-Weimar-Eisenach.* 2 vols. (Philadelphia: Carey, Lea & Carey, 1828).
6. Friedrich Schmidt, *Versuch über den politischen Zustand der Vereinigten Staaten* (Stuttgart; Tübingen: J.G. Cotta, 1822).
7. Samuel Cumings, *The Western Navigator; Containing Charts of the Ohio River… and of the Mississippi River, from the Mouth of the Missouri to the Gulf of Mexico…* (Philadelphia: E. Littell, 1822).
8. John Kilbourn, *The Ohio Gazetteer: or, Topographical Dictionary, Containing a Description of the Several Counties, Towns [etc.]… in the State of Ohio…* (Columbus: J. Kilbourn, 1821).

9. Walter Wadepuhl, *Goethe's Interest in the New World* (Jena: Fromannsche Buchhandlung Walter Biedermann, 1934), p. 32.
10. Moritz von Fürstenwärther and Hans Christoph von Gagern, *Der Deutsche in Nord-Amerika* (Stuttgart; Tübingen: J.G. Cotta, 1818).
11. Ludwig Gall, *Meine Auswanderung nach den Vereinigten Staaten im Frühjahr 1819 und meine Rückkehr nach der Heimat im Winter 1820*. 2 vols. (Trier: F.A. Gall, 1822).
12. Gall, vol. 2, p. 54.
13. Gall, vol. 2, p. 307.
14. Fürstenwärther, p. 120.
15. Heinrich von Struve, *Beiträge zur Mineralogie und Geologie des nördlichen Amerika's. Nach Amerikanischen Zeitschriften bearbeitet* (Hamburg: Perthes & Besser, 1822).

Carl Friedrich Zelter Travels for Goethe

1. A fortress and city on the Serbian Danube (today Petrovaradin).
2. Johann Wolfgang von Goethe and Joseph Sebastian Grüner, *Briefwechsel und mündlicher Verkehr zwischen Goethe und dem Rathe Grüner* (Leipzig: Gustav Mayer, 1853), p. 103–4.

Beyond the Chinese Wall to "World Poetry" and "World Literature"

1. Marco Polo, *Reise in den Orient während der Jahre 1272 bis 1295*, ed. Felix Peregrin (Ronneburg; Leipzig: Schumann, 1802).
2. Chrétien-Louis-Joseph de Guignes, *Voyages à Péking, Manille et l'Ile de France*. 3 vols. (Paris: Imprimerie Impériale, 1808).
3. *Hwa tseen ke, Chinese Courtship in Verse. To Which is Added, an Appendix, Treating of the Revenue of China*, transl. Peter Perring Thoms (Macao; London: East India Company; Parbury, Allen, and Kingsbury, 1824); *Iu kiao li, ou Les deux cousines*, transl. Jean-Pierre Abel-Rémusat. 4 vols. (Paris: Moutardier, 1826); *Contes chinois*, transl. François X. d'Entrecolles, John F. Davis and Peter P. Thoms (Paris: Moutardier, 1827).
4. Thomas Carlyle, *German Romance: Specimens of its Chief Authors, with Biographical and Critical Notices*. 4 vols. (Edinburgh: William Tait; London: Charles Tait 1827).
5. Thomas Carlyle, *Leben Schillers: aus dem Englischen eingeleitet durch Goethe* (Frankfurt a.M.: H. Wilmans, 1830). This German translation with a preface by Goethe was edited by the Berlin Society for Foreign Literature.

The Last Trip to Italy

1. August von Goethe, *Auf einer Reise nach Süden: Tagebuch 1830*, ed. Andreas Beyer and Gabriele Radecke (München; Wien: Hanser, 1999).

Further Reading

Bernhard, Duke of Saxe-Weimar-Eisenach. *Travels through North America, During the Years 1825 and 1826 by His Highness, Bernhard, Duke of Saxe-Weimar-Eisenach*. 2 vols. Philadelphia: Carey, Lea & Carey, 1828.

Boerner, Peter. *Goethe*. Transl. Nancy Boerner. 2d, rev. ed. London: Haus Publishing, 2013.

Boyd, James. *Goethe's Knowledge of English Literature*. New York: Haskell House Publishers, 1973.

Boyle, Nicholas. *Goethe. The Poet and the Age. Vol. 1: The Poetry of Desire, 1749–1790*. Oxford: Oxford University Press, 1991; *Vol. 2: Revolution and Renunciation, 1790–1803*. Oxford: Clarendon Press, 2000.

Bruford, Walter. *Culture and Society in Classical Weimar, 1775–1806*. Cambridge; London: Cambridge University Press, 1975.

The Cambridge Companion to Goethe. Ed. Lesley Sharpe. Cambridge, UK; New York: Cambridge University Press, 2002.

Conversations of Goethe with Johann Peter Eckermann. Transl. John Oxenford; ed. J.K. Moorhead. New York: Da Capo Press, 1998.

Forster, Georg. *A Voyage Round the World*. Ed. Nicholas Thomas and Oliver Berghof. 2 vols. Honolulu: University of Hawaii Press, 2000.

Goethe, Johann Wolfgang von. *Goethe's Collected Works*. Ed. Victor Lange, Eric Blackall and Cyrus Hamlin. 12 vols. New York: Suhrkamp, 1983–89; re-issue Princeton: Princeton University Press, 1994–96. Comprises:

Conversations of German Refugees. Transl. Jan van Heurck in cooperation with Jane K. Brown. *Wilhelm Meister's Journeyman Years, or, The Renunciants*. Ed. Jane K. Brown; transl. Krishna Winston.

Early Verse Drama and Prose Plays. Ed. Cyrus Hamlin and Frank Ryder; transl. Robert M. Browning [et al.].

Essays on Art and Literature. Ed. John Gearey; transl. Ellen von Nardroff and Ernest H. von Nardroff.

Faust I & II. Ed. and transl. Stuart Atkins.

From My Life: Poetry and Truth. Ed. Jeffrey L. Sammons and Thomas P. Saine; transl. Robert Heitner. 2 vols.

Italian Journey. Ed. Thomas P. Saine and Jeffrey L. Sammons; transl. Robert R. Heitner.

Scientific Studies. Ed. and transl. Douglas Miller.

Selected Poems. Ed. Christopher Middleton; transl. Michael Hamburger [et al.].

The Sorrows of Young Werther; Elective Affinities; Novella. Ed. David E. Wellbery; transl. Victor Lange and Judith Ryan.

Verse Plays and Epic. Ed. Cyrus Hamlin and Frank Ryder; transl. Michael Hamburger, Hunter Hannum and David Luke.

Wilhelm Meister's Apprenticeship. Ed. and transl. Eric A. Blackall in cooperation with Victor Lange.

——*Faust. Part One and Part Two*. The Bayard Taylor translation, rev. and ed. by Stuart Atkins. 2 vols. New York: Collier Books, 1962 and 1967. (This translation reflects the original metre.)

——*Faust. Parts One and Two*. Transl. and with an introduction by David Luke. 2 vols. Oxford: Oxford University Press, 2008.

——*Goethe, the Lyrist. 100 Poems*. Transl. Edwin Zeydel. 2d, rev. ed. New York: AMS Press, 1979.

——*Letters from Goethe*. Transl. M. von Herzfeld and C. Melvil Sym. Edinburgh: Edinburgh University Press, 1957.

——*Selected Poetry*. Transl. and with an introduction by David Luke. London: Penguin, 2005.

——*The Permanent Goethe*. Ed. and with an introduction by Thomas Mann. New York: Dial Press, 1948.

——*The Sorrows of Young Werther*. Transl. David Constantine. Oxford, UK; New York: Oxford University Press, 2012.

——*West-East Divan. The Poems, with "Notes and Essays": Goethe's Intercultural Dialogues*. Transl. Martin Bidney. Albany: State University of New York, 2010.

——*Wilhelm Meister*. Transl. H.M. Waidson. Richmond, Surrey: One World Classics, 2011. Contains *Wilhelm*

Meister's Years of Apprenticeship (*Wilhelm Meisters Lehrjahre*) and *Wilhelm Meister's Years of Travel* (*Wilhelm Meisters Wanderjahre*).

Goethe and the English-Speaking World. Ed. Nicholas Boyle and John Guthrie. Rochester, NY: Camden House, 2002.

Goethe Yearbook. Yearly Publication of the Goethe Society of North America. Rochester, NY; Woodbridge, UK: Camden House, 1982–.

Humboldt, Alexander von, and Aimé Bonpland. *Essay on the Geography of Plants*. Ed. Stephen T. Jackson; transl. Sylvie Romanowski. Chicago; London: University of Chicago Press, 2009.

Humboldt, Alexander von. *Political Essay on the Island of Cuba*. Ed. Vera M. Kutzinski and Ottmar Ette; transl. J. Bradford Anderson, Vera M. Kutzinski and Anja Becker. Chicago; London: University of Chicago Press, 2011.

——*Views of the Cordilleras, and Monuments of the Indigenous Peoples of the Americas*. Ed. Vera M. Kutzinski and Ottmar Ette; transl. J. Ryan Poynter. Chicago; London: University of Chicago Press, 2012.

——*Views of Nature*. Ed. Stephen T. Jackson and Laura Dassow Walls; transl. Mark W. Person. Chicago; London: University of Chicago Press, 2014.

Martius, Carl Friedrich Philipp von. *The Book of Palms – Das Buch der Palmen – Le livre des palmiers*. Ed. H. Walter Lack. Cologne: Taschen, 2010.

Publications of the English Goethe Society. Journal of the English Goethe Society published three times per year. Leeds: W.S. Maney & Son Ltd., 1924–.
Pückler-Muskau, Prince Hermann von. *Letters of a Dead Man*. Ed. and transl. Linda B. Parshall. Cambridge, Mass.: Harvard University Press, 2016.
Reed, T.J. *The Classical Centre: Goethe and Weimar, 1775–1832*. Oxford, UK; New York: Oxford University Press, 1986.
Said, Edward W. *Orientalism*. New York: Vintage Books, 2003.
Southey, Robert. *History of Brazil*. 3 vols. London: Longman, Hurst (et. al.), 1800–19.
Wied-Neuwied, Prince Maximilian of. *The North American Journals of Prince Maximilian of Wied*. Ed. Stephen S. Witte and Marsha V. Gallagher; transl. William J. Orr, Paul Schach and Dieter Karch. 3 vols. Omaha, Nebraska: Joslyn Art Museum, 2008, 2010, 2012.
——*Travels in Brazil in the Years 1815, 1816, 1817*. London: Henry Colburn & Co., 1820.
Williams, John R. *The Life of Goethe. A Critical Biography*. Oxford, UK; Malden, Mass.: Blackwell Publishers, 2001.
Wulf, Andrea. *The Invention of Nature: Alexander von Humboldt's New World*. New York: Alfred A. Knopf, 2015.

Image Credits

Figure 1: Klassik Stiftung Weimar, Sigrid Geske
Figure 2: "Goethes Kutsche@Goethes Wohnhaus Weimar" by Hajotthu is licensed under CC BY-SA 3.0
Figure 3: Courtesy Frankfurter Goethe-Haus
Figure 4: Beinecke Rare Book and Manuscript Library, Yale University
Figure 7: © Freies Deutsches Hochstift/Frankfurter Goethe-Museum
Figure 8: David Rumsey Map Collection. www.davidrumsey.com
Figure 9: Thüringer Universitäts- und Landesbibliothek Jena, 8 Geogr.I,87 : 41.1813
Figure 10: Image from the Biodiversity Heritage Library. Digitized by Smithsonian Libraries. www.biodiversitylibrary.org
Figure 11: By permission of the British Library, shelfmark BLL01002405846
Figure 12: Klassik Stiftung Weimar, unknown artist
Figure 13: Courtesy Lilly Library, Indiana University, Bloomington, Indiana
Figure 14: Courtesy Frankfurter Goethe-Haus
Figure 15: Courtesy Frankfurter Goethe-Haus

Figure 16: By permission of the British Library, shelfmark BLL01016750793